W9-APN-938

NO FUSS VEGAN

NO FUSS VEGAN

Everyday Food For Everyone

ROZ PURCELL

PENGUIN

IRELAND

PENGUIN IRELAND

UK | USA | Canada | Ireland | Australia
India | New Zealand | South Africa

Penguin Ireland is part of the Penguin Random House group of companies
whose addresses can be found at global.penguinrandomhouse.com.

Penguin
Random House
UK

First published 2020

001

Copyright © Roz Purcell, 2020

The moral right of the author has been asserted

Book design by Hart Studio
Photography by Joanne Murphy
Food and prop styling by Sarah-Kim Watchorn

Colour reproduction by Altaimage Ltd
Printed in China by RR Donnelley

A CIP catalogue record for this book is available from the British Library

ISBN: 978-1-844-88419-3

MIX
Paper from
responsible sources
FSC® C018179
FSC
www.fsc.org

ABOUT THE AUTHOR

Roz Purcell is a bestselling cookery author and superstar of the wellness scene.

A country girl from Tipperary, Roz first came to prominence when she won Miss Universe Ireland, but it wasn't until she quit modelling and launched her hugely popular food blog, Natural Born Feeder, that her career in recipe creation really took off. She gained a deeper understanding of what she should be eating pre- and post-workout, and began posting her recipes and workout tips on her website, quickly realising that there was huge demand for the kind of knowledge and inspiration she could offer.

Her childhood on her parents' farm – surrounded by nature and forever in the kitchen with her grandmother, cooking with local ingredients – still underpins her approach to her health. Balancing cooking and exercising has never been a chore, it's just a way of life. Roz has previously published two books, *Natural Born Feeder* and *Half Hour Hero*.

CONTENTS

INTRODUCTION

I can't believe this is my third cookbook. You might think it gets easier, but in fact the pressure to live up to previous popular recipes and books is a big challenge. That's why I gave myself three years between my last book, *Half Hour Hero*, and this one to get as much feedback as I could about what you wanted in my next book. Vegan recipes were what people wanted to see more of, so here's a whole book for you guys. I've been testing – and retesting! – the recipes and giving myself enough time to have my MacGyver moments in the kitchen and, well, sampling it all (it's a tough job, but someone has to do quality control!) to bring you over 100 new recipes to get you cooking and excited about what's for dinner or in your lunchbox.

Even though I asked my readers what they wanted for my next book, my books have always mirrored my own personal journey with food so it was a happy coincidence that in the past two years, I've shifted towards eating a more plant-based diet. When I first started Natural Born Feeder, I created a mission statement to help guide me and establish my values for NBF. As part of that mission statement I said that I don't advocate a certain type of diet. I love experimenting with vegan, vegetarian, gluten-free, raw recipes and so on. I am by no means 'anti' any food groups and I appreciate that people will have differing requirements for their way of living – food is so personal and specific to the individual that one size can never fit all. Although this book is called *No Fuss Vegan*, it's not just for people who follow a vegan diet – it's a book for anyone who simply wants to eat more vegetables and enjoy tasty meals in an easy, no-fuss way.

Why the change?

Bear with me for a minute as I fill you in on what's been happening in my life, as a lot has changed in the past three years. First of all, I'm now living by the Irish sea after thinking I would never give up my city lifestyle, but I travel to London a lot for work so I'm still getting the city experience but on an even bigger scale than Dublin. I feel like I'm balanced out by living two polar opposite lives.

I qualified as a personal trainer, which is something I did for myself and I'm so happy I did. I always had a fear of taking time out, but I realised that if it's something you're passionate about, it's worth it.

I started a hiking community called The Hike Life to share my love of hiking and introduce people to new routes and the benefits of getting out into nature at the weekends and exploring Ireland's fantastic trails.

And I started eating a more plant-based diet.

You're probably wondering what made me change my diet. I didn't have an epiphany or stop eating meat after I watched the latest Netflix documentary on becoming vegan. Years ago, I was adamant that I would never give up meat. Anyone who knows me or follows me on Twitter may remember that I even included the word carnivore in my bio – that's how much I loved eating meat.

I didn't consciously try to change; it just sort of happened. I was cooking my meals like I always had, where I based my plate around my meat or chicken, but I started to notice that I was leaving food behind – and if you know me at all, you know how strange that is. I just didn't enjoy eating meat any more. My taste for it was gone and eventually I preferred plant-based meals. After this I started to open my mind a little more to the environmental side of things too, which cemented my decision to stop eating meat and I haven't looked back.

I went fully vegan for a few months but then went back to being a vegetarian and have gone back and forth a few times since then. I never looked to change; I just do what suits me and eat what makes me happy. I'm not one of those people who judges others for how they eat, so don't expect a big lecture from me on why you need to stop eating a certain way or why you should alter your lifestyle. I think you should eat what makes you feel good and what you enjoy, but while you're at it, try eating lots of vegetables. The delicious recipes in this book are here to help you add more veggie-based meals into your diet, not completely change it. It's always fun to experiment with your food and try new meals, as you never know what you might discover, but if you're happy with your lifestyle as it is and you just want more ideas for how to eat your five a day, this is the book for you.

Look at your plate differently

Which brings me to my dad. He didn't want to change his diet completely. He decided that he liked the idea of being vegan at home, but that when he was out he would order whatever he wanted, whether it was a fish or veggie dish.

My dad timed his transition well, while I was at home to sit my driving test (I know, I know, I left that one a while, but don't worry, I passed!). I suspected that his idea of wanting to try a plant-based diet was a ploy to get me to cook for him for the two weeks I was at home, but nevertheless I used him as my guinea pig to test new recipes – my family is the best for honest feedback! After the two weeks were up, not only did my dad love not having to cook, but he also loved chickpea scramble. I never thought a former beef farmer from Tipperary would be so into a chickpea wrap!

Looking back, I think one of the funniest things about the whole experience was that my dad even changed his cup of tea. In our house, tea is sacrosanct and is made only one way – strong, with lashings of milk – so whenever I went home for a visit I usually had to bring a little carton of oat milk with me. After a while, though, he started to drink tea made with my oat milk and found that he actually preferred it. The fridge is like a shrine to oat milk now, which is handy for me.

I've dedicated a special recipe in this book to my dad after he sent me a request one day to make him a vegan black pudding. Not the simplest of tasks, but I was intrigued. It was the one thing he missed cooking for the Sunday fry-up and he's never asked me for a recipe for anything else, so I had to try it. See page 44 for the recipe – he LOVES it! That recipe is for my dad, but this book is full of alternative recipes that you all requested on Instagram, so here you go, over 100 tasty reasons to eat veggie tonight.

Eating a vegan diet can sometimes be misconceived as difficult, expensive, time-consuming and limiting, but I want to show you that it's none of those things. The recipes in this book will give you easy ways to eat more vegetables, help you to get creative with your food and will get you to look at your plate differently. Whether you want to make one vegan meal a day or even just one a week, I hope this book helps you to make easy, tasty recipes that fit into your lifestyle.

How to introduce more
plant-based meals

The question I probably get asked the most is, 'What diet do you follow?' The answer is easy: I eat what I enjoy and these days that happens to be mostly plant-based food. I don't feel the need to attach myself to any one label and I don't think you should either. To use a new term, I see myself as being quite flexi with food.

I'm not going to try to convince you to eat a certain way or change your whole lifestyle. Instead, I want to share some tips on how I approached eating more plants that might help anyone who is interested in shifting their eating habits. The recipes in this book will help you to shake up your normal cooking routine, entice you to try something new or just add more vegetables into your diet.

The idea of completely flipping my life around or eliminating things from my diet doesn't appeal to me at all. In fact, I find it overwhelming. The pressure to keep in line or not be tempted by 'bad' foods is not part of my relationship with food. I've always been a big fan of the dribble approach when it comes to any lifestyle changes, and by that I mean taking on a little at a time and adjusting over a longer period.

Here are some ways I started my journey.

TAKE IT ONE MEAL AT A TIME

In the past I've taken the all-or-nothing approach. Maybe that suits you but I've learned that it doesn't work for me, so I started by introducing one plant-based meal at a time. For you that might be one meal a day or one meal a week. I started to enjoy those meals more than my meat-based ones and I realised I had naturally created an appetite for plant-based meals. I suggest starting off by trying one new plant-based recipe a week, whether it's from this book or somewhere else. Before you know it, by the end of the month you'll have made four new recipes to add to your repertoire.

PLAN, STOCK UP AND PLAN AGAIN

This is always my advice when it comes to food! Planning has been fundamental to my journey. Because I was so used to cooking a certain way, I didn't have to put much thought into planning my meals. That all changed when I swapped to a plant-based diet, though. You would think that since I'm so comfortable with cooking it wouldn't be such a big deal, but it definitely was at the start, so don't feel like you're alone if you're struggling too. Meal planning involves having a good supply of ingredients at home and making the experience of cooking as efficient as possible (see the 'Inside my pantry' section on page 16 for what I always have on hand). I think social media, blogs and cookbooks really help with this. Bookmark recipes online or in a book or save photos on Instagram, then think of this as your mini catalogue when choosing your meals for the week ahead.

FIND WHAT YOU LOVE

When it comes to food, I like to think in terms of adding rather than eliminating – in other words, don't concentrate on what you can't have, but rather, look at everything that you can. There is a general misconception that a plant-based diet can be boring, but you'll probably start discovering so many new foods. By exploring more plant-based options, I've even found some new favourites. Some alternatives have really blown me away, such as oat milk, jackfruit and nut cheese, and I now enjoy eating or drinking them more than the versions I was eating before. Finding the foods that you like and that suit you is trial and error. You'll probably notice that some typical vegan foods, such as tempeh and seitan, are missing from this book, either because I didn't particularly like them or because they aren't widely available – like anything else, it comes down to individual preference. Keeping a simple food diary of what you really enjoyed and things that agreed with you is a good place to start.

FIND PLANT-BASED VERSIONS OF YOUR FAVOURITE FOODS

With a constant stream of food pictures delivered straight to our screens, we can get a bit overwhelmed with feeling like we need to eat what other people do. Eat the food that suits you and fits into your lifestyle. I found that creating vegan versions of things I love, like meringues or buttery shortbread, was a huge help, so I suggest that you do the same. Whether you have a craving for shepherd's pie or you fancy a cheesecake, finding plant-based versions of your old favourites is a fantastic way to get excited about making a new recipe.

FIND THE LITTLE THINGS THAT HELP

Finding that small addition that adds loads of flavour, such as miso paste, sriracha or nutritional yeast, or having things in your kitchen that make your life easier, such as a food processor, high-speed blender and good knives, really does make a difference. Whatever helps to make your food taste better and make your life easier will help you to make the switch to a plant-based diet.

INSIDE MY PANTRY

A well-stocked pantry is a fundamental part of preparation and making cooking convenient. Here's a basic list of what you'll find in my cupboards.

SPICES, CONDIMENTS AND FLAVOURINGS

A small amount of any of these can add a huge boost to flavour.

SPICES

- *Basil*
- *Bay leaves*
- *Chilli powder*
- *Cinnamon*
- *Coriander*
- *Cumin*
- *Curry powder*
- *Oregano*
- *Paprika*
- *Rosemary*
- *Sea salt*
- *Thyme*
- *Turmeric*

CONDIMENTS AND FLAVOURINGS

- *Chilli paste*
- *Miso paste*
- *Sriracha hot sauce*
- *Tamari or soy sauce*
- *Tomato purée*
- *Vegan Worcestershire sauce*
- *Vinegar (apple cider or rice)*

SWEETENERS

I've always loved using sweeteners that are as natural and unrefined as possible and I also love the taste. They don't overpower the recipe and a little goes a long way.

- *Apple sauce*
- *Coconut sugar*
- *Dried fruit*
- *Maple syrup*

GRAINS AND PASTA

- *Oats*
- *Pasta*
- *Quinoa*
- *Rice*
- *Rice noodles*

STASHED IN THE CUPBOARDS

I'm a huge fan of having beans and lentils ready to go, especially midweek. So if you're like me, opt for jarred or tinned beans and lentils for convenience.

- *Beans: chickpeas, kidney beans, cannellini beans, black beans*
- *Dried fruit: dates, raisins, apricots, figs*
- *Lentils: green, brown, dried red split lentils*

- Nut butters
- Nuts: all kinds
- Oil: olive, almond, coconut, sesame
- Seeds: flax, chia, sesame
- Tahini
- Tinned chopped tomatoes
- Tinned jackfruit

FLOURS AND BAKING SUPPLIES

I have nothing against white flour, but there are so many recipes out there that use it. I like the challenge of creating recipes with alternatives like these.

- Baking powder
- Bicarbonate of soda
- Chickpea flour
- Oat flour
- Quinoa flour

FREEZER

You'll never go hungry if you have a well-stocked freezer. A huge amount of my food prep is kept in the freezer for ease throughout the week.

- Acai
- Banana slices
- Berries: freezing them is the only way they'll keep, especially during the summer months. Frozen berries are still perfect for adding to smoothies, making chia jam and even as nibbles.
- Bread: I keep slices in the freezer so that I can toast only what I need – and to stop me from eating the entire loaf for fear it will go off!

- Ice
- Peas
- Peeled and chopped veg in reusable freezerproof bags
- Steamed cauliflower
- Sweetcorn

STRANGER THINGS, EXPLAINED

Here's more information about some stranger things you may not have come across before.

- Agar agar: a Japanese setting agent. It's a vegetable alternative to gelatine and is available in health food stores or the Asian section of some supermarkets.
- Nutritional yeast: sometimes referred to as 'vegan crack', this is the flaky stuff that almost looks like fish food. It gives sauces and dressings a cheesy flavour. It's mostly found in health food shops or supermarkets with a well-stocked health food aisle.
- Vegan protein powder: there are so many on the market, but finding your favourite can be hard. From pea to hemp, rice or soy, they all have their own unique taste. I love adding a scoop to my morning shake or porridge for a quick hit of protein and for making high-protein treats.

BREAKFAST

First things first!

I'm an early riser, which I think comes from growing up on a farm. Even when I didn't have jobs to do, the noise of my dad banging around the kitchen making his first cup of tea or my mum calling the cats and dogs to feed couldn't be ignored. These days I like getting up before everyone else and having that time to myself before the chaos of the day begins. No one is emailing or calling me and there's not much activity online.

My morning ritual is what sets me up for the day – a walk with my dog, Willay, up Killiney Hill just as it gets bright, a strong cup of tea and breakfast in silence. It's like my reset and I may as well enjoy it until I have kids!

As for my favourite breakfasts? Well, if you know me at all then it won't come as a shock when I say it has to be the chickpea scramble for a savoury morning or proats for a breakfast on the go. At the weekend it's a toss-up between the vegan fry-up, corn fritters or simple oat pancakes. And I make the homemade Notella on repeat!

BAKED OATMEAL

For those of you who don't use protein powder, which I use in my proats
recipe (page 30), here is a yummy baked oats dish with all the glory
of a dessert – breakfast made with simple everyday goodness.

oil, for greasing

2 tbsp chia seeds or
milled flaxseeds

6 tbsp water

3 small to medium
overripe bananas (the
more brown spots, the
better!)

250g porridge oats

2 handfuls of mixed
seeds

250ml non-dairy milk

zest and juice of ½ an
orange (optional)

4 tbsp maple syrup

1 tbsp ground cinnamon
(add more if you
love cinnamon)

150g mixed berries

handful of fresh
blueberries

To serve:

soy or coconut yogurt

almond butter

Preheat the oven to 180°C. Grease an ovenproof dish.

Put the chia seeds or milled flaxseeds and water in a small
bowl and stir to combine. Set aside to soak for 15 minutes.

Mash the bananas in a large bowl. Add the soaked chia or
flaxseeds along with the oats, seeds, milk, orange zest and
juice (if using), maple syrup and cinnamon. Mix well, then
stir in the mixed berries.

Pour the mix into the greased dish and scatter the extra
blueberries on top. Bake in the preheated oven for 45 minutes.

This is perfect for prepping the night before to heat up later
(it will keep in the fridge for up to three days), but if you're
like me and you can't wait, you can dig in straight away. Serve
with a dollop of yogurt and almond butter on top.

GRANOLA

This crunchy granola is so good that I have to hide it from myself when I make a batch! It makes the perfect snack served with ice-cold coconut milk or as a quick topping for a summer crumble or smoothie bowl.

300g oats (porridge, rolled or jumbo oats will all work; or use brown rice flakes or a quinoa/millet mix if you want this to be gluten-free)

150g nuts, roughly chopped (or you could use seeds instead of nuts or a mix of both)

50g flaxseeds

50g coconut flakes

pinch of sea salt

5 tbsp maple syrup

4 tbsp coconut or olive oil (or opt for canola oil for a neutral flavour)

80g dried fruit, such as cranberries, goji berries and/or chopped dates

60g cacao nibs

Preheat the oven to 170°C.

Put the oats, nuts, flaxseeds, coconut and salt in a large bowl and stir to combine.

Put the maple syrup and oil in a small pan over a medium heat and melt together. Pour over the dry ingredients and stir to coat.

Tip onto a large baking tray and spread it out evenly. Bake in the preheated oven for 25 minutes.

Remove from the oven and stir in the dried fruit and cacao nibs. Allow to cool completely, then store in a large glass jar or airtight container.

GRANOLA BARS

These have a really nice soft centre with a crunchy outside. You can tweak these to suit your tastes by adding dried fruit or chocolate chips, but they're delicious simply as they are here, paired with a cuppa on the go.

2 tbsp milled flaxseeds

6 tbsp water

200g porridge oats

120g hazelnuts or almonds, chopped (or blend for a few seconds to break down into small chunks)

1 tsp ground cinnamon

pinch of sea salt

4 tbsp maple syrup

2 tbsp peanut butter

1 tbsp coconut oil

3 tbsp unsweetened almond milk

1 tsp vanilla extract

Preheat the oven to 180°C. Line a 15cm square baking tin with non-stick baking paper.

Put the milled flaxseeds and water in a small bowl and stir to combine. Set aside to soak for 15 minutes.

Meanwhile, put the oats, nuts, cinnamon and salt in a large bowl and stir to combine.

Put the maple syrup, peanut butter and coconut oil in a small saucepan over a medium heat and melt together. Remove from the heat and stir in the almond milk, vanilla and the flax 'egg', then pour over the dry ingredients and stir to combine.

Tip the mix into the lined tin, pressing the top down evenly. Bake in the preheated oven for 35 minutes. Allow to cool fully in the tin before gently lifting out and cutting into eight bars. Store in an airtight container for up to six days.

OVERNIGHT OATS

Breakfast on the go never tasted so good with these easy
ways to prep a delicious bowl the night before.

GET YOUR GREENS

1 banana, peeled

handful of spinach leaves

200ml nut milk (if you're
not using the protein
powder, use only
150ml nut milk)

1 tbsp maple syrup or
4 green grapes, for
sweetness

40g porridge oats

30g vegan vanilla protein
powder (optional)

Put the banana, spinach, nut milk and maple syrup or grapes in a blender and blitz until smooth. Stir in the oats and protein powder (if using), then pour into a bowl or jar and let it sit overnight in the fridge. Eat cold straight from the fridge the next day or heat it up.

CHOCO BLOCK

40g porridge oats or
4 tbsp chia seeds

40g vegan chocolate
protein powder

200ml nut milk

1 tbsp almond or
peanut butter

Put all the ingredients in a bowl or jar and stir to combine, then let it sit overnight in the fridge. Eat cold straight from the fridge the next day or heat it up.

COCONUT BIRCHER

20g porridge oats

½ a Pink Lady apple,
grated (optional)

200ml coconut milk
from a carton

2 tbsp coconut yogurt
(or more coconut milk)

2 tbsp flaxseeds

2 tbsp mixed seeds

1 tbsp chia seeds

1 tbsp maple syrup

Put all the ingredients in a bowl or jar and stir to combine, then let it sit overnight in the fridge. Eat cold straight from the fridge the next day or heat it up.

Serves 5

SUPER SEEDY PORRIDGE MIX

For a porridge with a little more oomph, feel free to add some vanilla protein powder or mashed banana here for an extra-creamy bowl.

100g porridge oats
50g sunflower seeds
30g flaxseeds
30g chia seeds
2 tbsp sesame seeds
pinch of sea salt
200ml nut milk per
*   portion, to cook*

For the caramelised
** bananas (per portion):**
1 banana, sliced
*   lengthways*
1 tbsp maple syrup, plus
*   extra for serving*

To serve:
hemp seeds

Put the oats, seeds and salt in a bowl and mix to combine, then store in a large clean jar.

When you want to cook the porridge, put 40g of the porridge mix in a saucepan with the nut milk. Bring to a steady simmer and cook for 4 to 5 minutes. Add more milk for a less stodgy bowl.

Meanwhile, make your caramelised bananas. This is my favourite topping for porridge – not every day, but on a lazy Sunday morning, it's the nicest treat. Start by heating a non-stick frying pan over a medium-high heat. Add the banana slices to the pan and drizzle over the maple syrup. Cook for 2 to 3 minutes on each side, until golden around the edges and softened just a tad – you don't want them to be falling apart.

To serve, transfer the cooked porridge to a bowl. Carefully lift the bananas out of the pan onto the porridge. Scatter over the hemp seeds and don't forget any leftover maple syrup from the pan, plus an extra drizzle – yum!

PROATS

This is probably the recipe that's featured the most on my Instagram feed. I am addicted to proats – the texture is like bread meets cake. You'll never look back once you start making this for breakfast. It's the kind of meal that will have you counting down the hours until morning, although I sometimes have this for dinner too!

1 small banana (100g)

40g porridge oats

40g vegan protein powder
(I recommend chocolate)

170ml non-dairy milk

75g berries (blueberries, strawberries or raspberries)

To serve:

coconut yogurt

chopped nuts

fresh strawberries

Preheat the oven to 180°C.

Mash the banana in a bowl, then add the oats, protein powder and milk. Stir well to ensure the protein powder is fully mixed in and there are no lumps. Fold in the berries.

Pour the mix into a small oven dish, such as a 1lb loaf tin or a 10cm round cake tin. Bake in the preheated oven for 25 minutes. Allow to cool, then leave to set overnight in the fridge.

Enjoy for breakfast the next day with coconut yogurt, chopped nuts and strawberries.

CAULI-POWER SMOOTHIE BOWL

Yep, you read that right, a cauliflower smoothie.
Cauliflower really is the most versatile of foods!

1 small cauliflower

250g frozen raspberries
or strawberries

80g of vegan protein
powder

150ml unsweetened
almond milk

2 tbsp maple syrup (if
using an unflavoured
protein powder)

To serve:

your favourite smoothie
bowl toppings

First you need to steam and freeze the cauliflower. To do this, remove and discard the stem and break the head into small florets. Steam until tender, then allow to cool completely before putting the florets into freezer bags. Store for up to three weeks in the freezer.

When you're ready to make the smoothie bowl, combine all the ingredients in a high-speed blender and blend until super-smooth. The mix will be very thick, like soft-serve ice cream.

Spoon into a bowl and top with your favourite bits. I like peanut butter, raspberries and cacao nibs.

ACAI BOWL

This vibrant bowl will start your day with some vibrant colour.
Creamy and soft, perfect for a summer morning.

1 banana

1 x 100g packet of acai

100g frozen blueberries

40g vegan protein powder (optional)

100ml non-dairy milk

1 tbsp maple syrup (not necessary if your protein powder is sweetened)

1 tbsp peanut butter

To serve:

banana slices

kiwi slices

fresh blueberries

fresh coconut shavings

handful of granola (page 23)

You'll need to prep this the night before by peeling and dicing your banana, then popping into a reusable food bag or bowl and freezing.

In the morning, combine all the ingredients in a high-speed blender and blend until super-smooth. The mix will be very thick, like soft serve ice cream.

Spoon into a bowl and add your favourite toppings. I use banana, kiwi, blueberries, coconut and a handful of my crunchy granola.

NA NA BREAKFAST BOWL

Soft-serve meets smoothie with this ultimate creamy bowl that will make you feel like you're abroad. Just don't dig in too fast or it might give you brain freeze – I warned you! Feel free to add protein powder, some greens, such as spinach, or berries to give this bowl a deeper colour.

3 bananas
2 Medjool dates, pitted
100ml unsweetened almond milk
2 tbsp peanut butter

To serve:
Notella spread (page 58)
chopped peanuts

You'll need to prep this the night before by peeling and dicing your bananas, then popping into a reusable food bag or bowl and freezing.

In the morning, combine all the ingredients in a high-speed blender and blend until super-smooth. Drizzle some Notella chocolate spread into two small bowls, then spoon in the creamy mixture and top with chopped peanuts.

CHICKPEA SCRAMBLE

I even have my dad addicted to chickpea scramble. It's perfect for a
quick breakfast or lunch, loaded on avocado toast or rolled up in a wrap.
Nutritional yeast is an inactive yeast that has a super cheesy flavour.
You can get it in all health food stores and some supermarkets.

1 tsp avocado or olive oil

1 x 400g tin of chickpeas,
  drained and rinsed

2½ tbsp nutritional yeast

1 tsp ground cumin

½ tsp ground turmeric

½ tsp paprika

sea salt and freshly
  ground black pepper

To serve:

rye bread

cherry tomatoes

avocado

spring onions

chopped fresh herbs,
  such as basil or
  flat-leaf parsley

Heat the oil in a small or medium-sized saucepan over a
medium heat. Toss in the chickpeas. Using a potato masher
or fork, smash the chickpeas until they're broken down.
Stir in the nutritional yeast, spices and seasoning. Cook
for 2 to 3 minutes, stirring all the time.

Remove from the heat and serve with rye bread, cherry
tomatoes, avocado, spring onions and mixed herbs.

BANANA BREAKFAST MUFFINS

My favourite kind of breakfast – sweet! The smell of these muffins baking will help you to jump straight out of bed. This recipe makes eight muffins, but if you want to make 12 to fill a muffin tin, scale up the ingredients by 1.5.

oil, for greasing
2 tbsp milled flaxseeds
6 tbsp water
50g porridge oats
100g ground almonds
2 tsp ground cinnamon
1 tsp baking powder
½ tsp bicarbonate of soda
1 lemon
2 overripe bananas
3 tbsp nut milk
2 tbsp maple syrup
1 tsp vanilla extract
250g fresh or frozen blueberries
25g whole almonds, chopped

Preheat the oven to 180°C. Grease eight cups of a muffin tray with a little oil or use paper liners.

Start by combining the milled flaxseeds and water in a small bowl. Let it sit for 15 minutes to bulk up.

Meanwhile, blend the oats into a flour consistency and tip into a bowl along with the ground almonds, cinnamon, baking powder and bicarbonate of soda. Mix well.

Zest the lemon, then juice one half only.

In a separate bowl, mash the bananas, then stir in the soaked flaxseeds, lemon zest and juice, nut milk, maple syrup and vanilla. Pour the liquid mix into the dry ingredients and stir to combine into a thick, smooth batter. Fold in the blueberries.

Spoon the mix into the greased or lined muffin cups, then top with the chopped almonds. Bake in the preheated oven for 25 minutes. Leave to cool for 10 minutes before enjoying. Store in an airtight container in the fridge for up to four days.

CHICKPEA 'EGG' MUFFINS

These are a handy brekkie on the go or snack.

1 tbsp oil, plus extra
    for greasing

1 red onion, peeled and
    finely diced

½ a courgette, grated

100g spinach

14 sun-dried
    tomatoes, diced

200g chickpea flour

3 tbsp nutritional yeast
    (optional)

450ml water

sea salt and freshly
    ground black pepper

Preheat the oven to 190°C. Grease eight cups of a muffin tray with a little oil.

Heat the tablespoon of oil in a frying pan over a high heat. Toss in the diced onion and cook for 2 minutes, stirring constantly. Add the grated courgette, spinach and sun-dried tomatoes and cook for 1 minute, until the courgette and spinach have wilted. Remove from the heat and set aside.

Now for the batter. Put the chickpea flour in a medium-sized bowl along with the nutritional yeast (if using), salt and pepper. Pour in the water and whisk until the batter is smooth.

Add 2 tablespoons of the veg filling to each greased muffin cup. Pour over the chickpea batter, filling each cup up to the top. Bake in the preheated oven for 30 minutes.

Once cooked, remove the muffins from the tray and allow to cool on a wire rack before eating or storing in the fridge for up to three days.

Serves 2

QUINOA PANCAKES

Your lazy Saturday mornings are sorted. These are simply
delicious with nothing more than a drizzle of maple syrup.

*2 tbsp milled chia seeds
or milled flaxseeds*
6 tbsp water
100g quinoa flour
1 tsp baking powder
pinch of sea salt
150ml non-dairy milk
1 tbsp oil

Put the milled chia or flaxseeds and water in a small bowl
and stir to combine. Set aside to soak for 15 minutes.

Put the quinoa flour, baking powder, salt and milk in
a blender and blend until smooth, then stir through
the flax 'eggs'.

Heat half of the oil in a non-stick frying pan over a low
heat. Pour three small mounds of the batter into the pan.
Cook for 3 to 4 minutes, until risen. Flip over and cook
for another 4 minutes, until golden. Transfer to a plate
and keep warm.

Repeat with the remaining batter – you should get six
pancakes in total.

VEGAN FRY-UP

Dear Dad, this one's for you. You've waited long enough for
me to create a doppelgänger for your favourite Sunday dish.
I hope you guys enjoy it as much as my dad does!

**For the vegan
black pudding:**

1 tbsp oil

½ a red onion, peeled
and grated

1 small garlic clove,
peeled and crushed

1 tsp paprika

1 tsp allspice

½ x 400g tin of kidney
beans, drained and
rinsed

½ x 400g tin of black
beans, drained and
rinsed

40g porridge oats

1½ tbsp tamari or soy
sauce

1 tbsp vegan
Worcestershire sauce

sea salt and freshly
ground black pepper

**For the homemade
beans:**

1 x 400g tin of cannellini
beans, drained and
rinsed

250g tomato passata

1 tbsp tamari or soy
sauce

To make the vegan black pudding, heat the oil in a frying pan
over a high heat until it's sizzling. Add the onion and fry for
30 seconds, stirring constantly to ensure it doesn't burn.
Add the crushed garlic and spices and cook for 1 minute.
Remove from the heat and leave to one side for a moment.

Put the kidney beans and black beans in a blender and
blitz for 20 seconds. They should be broken down but not
completely smooth, with some parts of the beans still visible.

Scrape into a medium-sized bowl. Stir in the rest of the
ingredients, including the onion mix, and combine well.

Tear off a piece of baking paper. Tip the mixture out onto the
paper and roll into a long sausage shape, wrapping the baking
paper around it to mould it into shape. Slice into thick discs
if using it straight away or store in the fridge for up to three
days in the baking paper and cut off pieces as you need them.

To make the homemade beans, put all the ingredients in
a small saucepan over a high heat and combine well. Bring
to the boil, then reduce the heat and cook for 2 minutes.
Remove from the heat and keep warm until ready to serve.

To make the tofu scramble, heat the oil in a frying pan over
a medium heat. Add the tofu and use a fork to break it
up into small pieces, similar to how scrambled eggs look.
Add the nutritional yeast and spices and stir to combine,
making the tofu a vibrant yellow colour. Cook for 2 minutes.
Remove from the heat and stir in the spring onions.

1 tbsp maple syrup

1 tbsp tomato purée

1 tsp dried oregano

1 tsp paprika

For the tofu scramble:

1 tbsp oil

250g tofu

3 tbsp nutritional yeast

1 tbsp paprika

1 tsp ground turmeric

1 tsp ground cumin

2 spring onions, chopped

To serve:

quinoa bread (page 197)
   or seeded oat loaf
   (page 198)

grilled tomatoes

grilled mushrooms

sliced avocado

Serve the vegan black pudding, homemade beans and tofu scramble with bread, grilled tomatoes and mushrooms and sliced avocado for a complete fry-up.

FRENCH TOAST

Crisp on the outside, soft on the inside and drizzled with maple
syrup – it can only be the perfect French toast, vegan style.

300ml non-dairy milk
4 tbsp chickpea flour
1 tbsp ground cinnamon
1 tsp vanilla extract
4 thick slices of bread
2 tbsp oil

To serve:
coconut yogurt
fresh figs, quartered
3 tbsp maple syrup
*handful of toasted
    hazelnuts, roughly
    chopped*

Combine the non-dairy milk, chickpea flour, cinnamon and
vanilla in a blender and blitz until smooth. Pour into a wide
dish, then dip the slices of bread in the mixture one at a time,
making sure to coat both sides for 20 seconds each.

Heat the oil in a non-stick frying pan over a medium-high
heat. Add the bread and cook for 90 seconds on each side,
until golden and crisp along the edges.

To serve, divide the French toast between two plates. Top with
a dollop of coconut yogurt, scatter over the figs and drizzle
with the maple syrup, then top with the chopped hazelnuts.

Makes 8

SAVOURY WAFFLES

I do eat savoury things now and again, I promise! This simple favourite of mine
is a great substitute for toast when loaded up with mashed avocado or pesto.

1 tbsp chia seeds or
   milled flaxseeds

3 tbsp water

120g oat flour

150ml to 200ml almond,
   oat or soy milk

1 tbsp nutritional yeast
   (optional)

1½ tsp apple cider
   vinegar

1 tsp dried oregano

¼ tsp bicarbonate of
   soda

sea salt and freshly
   ground black pepper

oil, for greasing

To serve:

diced avocado

vegan basil pesto (page
   86)

chopped fresh herbs,
   such as chives, basil or
   flat-leaf parsley

Put the chia or flaxseeds and water in a small bowl and set
aside for 15 minutes to plump up.

Put the chia or flaxseed 'egg' in a blender along with all the
other ingredients except the oil and blitz to combine. Grease
your waffle iron with a little oil.

Add 3 to 4 tablespoons of the batter to your hot waffle iron.
Cook for about 4 minutes, depending on the temperature
and size of your waffle iron.

Repeat using the rest of the batter. You should have enough
to make eight small waffles.

Serve with diced avocado, pesto and chopped fresh herbs.

SIMPLE OAT PANCAKES

This really is a no-fuss stack. Whenever I've made these pancakes
for people, they can't get over how easy they are to make with so few
ingredients. Feel free to add a scoop of vegan protein powder to the mix.

250g oats (porridge,
  rolled or jumbo oats
  will all work)

2 bananas, peeled

400ml oat milk

handful of dark chocolate
  chips or raisins

1 tbsp oil

To serve:

coconut yogurt

chopped toasted hazelnuts

fresh strawberries

vegan chocolate shavings

maple syrup

Put the oats in a blender and blitz into a flour. Add the
bananas and milk and blend until smooth. Stir in the
chocolate chips or raisins.

Heat the oil in a non-stick frying pan over a high heat. Pour
tablespoons of batter into the pan (you should have room
in the pan for about five pancakes) and cook for 1 minute,
lowering the heat if necessary. Once the edges begin to lift
and the base is cooked, flip and cook for a further 30 seconds.
Repeat until all the batter is used up. You should have enough
to make 10 small pancakes.

Serve with coconut yogurt, toasted hazelnuts, strawberries and
chocolate shavings and drizzle everything with maple syrup.

VEGAN SHAKSHUKA

A warming savoury dish that's great for a cold morning. Shakshuka is also perfect for friends coming over for brunch or as a meal all for yourself.

1 tbsp paprika

1 tbsp ground cumin

1 tsp ground turmeric

1 tbsp oil

½ a red onion, thinly sliced

1 garlic clove, peeled and crushed

1 x 400g tin of chopped tomatoes

1 x 400g tin of cannellini beans, drained and rinsed

100g spinach, chopped

1 batch of chickpea scramble (page 38) or tofu scramble (page 45)

To serve:

sliced avocado

chopped spring onions

chopped fresh herbs

griddled or toasted sourdough bread

Combine the paprika, cumin and turmeric in a small bowl and set aside.

Heat the oil in a frying pan over a medium-high heat. Add the onion and cook for 2 minutes, then toss in the garlic and spices and cook for 1 minute more. Add the tomatoes, beans and spinach and cook for 2 minutes, until the spinach has wilted.

Make a few wells in the tomato mixture, then spoon in the chickpea or tofu scramble and cook until just heated through.

Scatter over the avocado, spring onions and herbs, then bring straight to the table to dish up. Serve with thick slices of griddled or toasted sourdough bread on the side.

CORN FRITTERS

These are delicious either hot or cold. They have so much flavour and are like little savoury crumpets. I love bringing them with me for a breakfast on the go.

80g chickpea flour

1 tbsp mild curry powder

1 tsp paprika

½ tsp ground turmeric

pinch of sea salt

150ml unsweetened almond milk

150g fresh or frozen sweetcorn

80g courgette, grated

40g carrot, peeled and grated

2 spring onions, chopped

1 tbsp oil

For the salsa:

8 cherry tomatoes, quartered

¼ red onion, finely diced

½ fresh green chilli, deseeded and finely diced

small bunch of fresh coriander, chopped

1 tbsp olive oil

To make the salsa, put all the ingredients in a bowl and stir gently to combine. Set aside to allow the flavours to marry together while you make the fritters.

Put the chickpea flour, curry powder, paprika, turmeric and salt in a small bowl and stir to combine, then whisk in the almond milk to create a smooth batter.

Put the sweetcorn, courgette, carrot and spring onions in a separate large bowl and stir to combine. Add the batter to the veggies and mix well.

Heat the oil in a frying pan over a high heat. Add about 2 tablespoons of the fritter mix to the pan, pressing it down with the back of the spoon to spread it out a little. Cook for 3 to 4 minutes on each side, until the edges are golden and crisp and the fritters are cooked through. You may need to lower the heat a little as you cook the fritters in batches so that you don't burn the last few.

Serve with spoonfuls of tomato salsa on top.

NOTELLA TOAST WITH FRUIT

I'd say take a wild guess what my favourite toast is, but I'm sure you've already figured it out. This rich hazelnut spread is made in seconds, so there's always a jar sitting in our fridge.

100g skinned hazelnuts,
  raw or toasted
100ml nut milk
4 tbsp maple syrup
2 tbsp cacao powder
pinch of sea salt

To serve:
slices of bread, toasted
fresh strawberries and
  other fresh berries
pinch of bee pollen

Put the hazelnuts, nut milk, maple syrup, cacao powder and salt in a high-speed blender and blitz until smooth. Spoon into a clean jar and store in the fridge for up to five days.

To serve, spread your toast thickly with the chocolate hazelnut spread and top with fresh berries and a pinch of bee pollen.

Makes 1 small jar each

of mascarpone and jam

TOAST WITH MASCARPONE AND BLACKBERRY JAM

This vegan mascarpone goes great with everything and anything – pancakes, cakes, muffins, biscuits, you name it. For a sweet breakfast to impress, definitely try this out.

For the mascarpone:

150g raw cashews
100ml nut milk
juice of 1 lime
2 tbsp maple syrup
1 tsp vanilla extract

For the blackberry jam:

250g fresh or frozen blackberries
2 tbsp chia seeds
2 tbsp maple syrup

To serve:

slices of bread, toasted
fresh basil leaves

To make the vegan mascarpone, put all the ingredients in a high-speed blender and blitz until you have a smooth, thick paste. Spoon into a clean jar and store in the fridge for up to five days.

To make the jam, put the berries in a small pan over a medium heat and cook for 4 to 5 minutes, stirring occasionally, until they've broken down into a thick, chunky sauce. Remove from the heat and stir in the chia seeds and maple syrup. Spoon into a clean jar or bowl and let it sit for 20 minutes to thicken into a lovely berry jam. Keep refrigerated for up to three days.

To serve, spread the mascarpone over your toast, then top with the blackberry jam and fresh basil leaves.

TOAST WITH PROTEIN ALMOND SPREAD, BANANA AND TOASTED SEEDS

This spread is like a thick vanilla nut butter. You'll never look back once you make this – I can't have almond butter any other way now.

20g vegan vanilla protein powder

2 tbsp almond butter

1 tbsp coconut oil

To serve:

1 slice of bread, toasted

1 banana, peeled and sliced

handful of seeds, toasted

Put all the ingredients in a small bowl and stir to combine into a smooth spread. Use immediately or store in the fridge for up to two days.

To serve, spread thickly on toast and top with the sliced banana and seeds.

Mascarpone and
Blackberry Jam

Protein Almond
Spread, Banana
and Toasted Seeds

Notella Toast with Fruit

Almond Ricotta
and Sweet Red Onion

TOAST WITH ALMOND RICOTTA AND SWEET RED ONION

I love this combination of the soft, sweet onion with the tangy ricotta on a crisp slice of toast. It makes a great breakfast, lunch or even starter.

1 tbsp oil
1 red onion, peeled
   and thinly sliced
1 tbsp maple syrup

For the almond ricotta:
100g blanched almonds
juice of 1 lemon
80ml unsweetened
   almond milk
2 tbsp nutritional yeast
pinch of sea salt

To serve:
1 slice of bread, toasted
freshly ground black pepper

To make the ricotta, put all the ingredients in a high-speed blender and blitz until smooth. Spoon into a clean jar and store in the fridge for up to three days.

Heat the oil in a frying pan over a high heat. Toss in the red onion and cook for 2 to 3 minutes, until the onion is slightly golden and crisp. Stir in the maple syrup and cook for a further 30 seconds, then remove from the heat.

To serve, spread the almond ricotta thickly on your toast, then top with the sweet red onion and some freshly ground black pepper.

WHITE BEAN AND AVOCADO TOAST

A different way to enjoy your avocado toast and change things up.

1 ripe avocado, peeled, stoned and halved

40g spinach, chopped

juice of 2 limes

1 tsp miso paste

1 x 400g tin of cannellini beans, drained and rinsed

2 spring onions, finely chopped

4 slices of bread, toasted

handful of sunflower seeds, toasted

Use a fork to mash the avocado in a medium-sized bowl. Add the spinach, lime juice and miso and mash together, then stir in the beans and spring onions.

Load onto the toast, then sprinkle over the seeds.

Makes 1 small jar

BAGELS WITH TOFU PESTO CREAM CHEESE

Bagels with cream cheese is a classic breakfast across the world. Make this cream cheese ahead of time and in an early morning rush you're laughing.

1 x 400g block of firm tofu

juice of 1 lemon

4 tbsp nutritional yeast

2 tbsp vegan basil pesto (page 86)

pinch of sea salt

To serve:

toasted bagels

Put all the ingredients in a high-speed blender and blitz until smooth. Spoon into a clean jar and store in the fridge for up to five days.

To serve, spread thickly on toasted halved bagels.

TOAST WITH ROAST PARSNIP HUMMUS AND MISO MUSHROOMS

The sweet roast parsnip hummus and the savoury miso mushrooms make such a great duo – you have to try it.

For the roast parsnip hummus:

2 large parsnips, peeled and diced

3 tbsp olive oil, plus extra for drizzling

1 tbsp balsamic vinegar

1 tbsp maple syrup

pinch of sea salt

1 x 400g tin of chickpeas, drained and rinsed

juice of 1 lemon

1 tbsp tahini

For the miso mushrooms:

1 tbsp oil

200g mushrooms of your choice, washed and stemmed (if needed) and sliced

1 tbsp tamari or soy sauce

1 tbsp maple syrup

2 tsp miso paste

To serve:

4 slices of bread, toasted

To garnish:

chopped fresh herbs

Preheat the oven to 200°C.

To make the hummus, put the parsnips in a large bowl. In a separate small bowl or jug, whisk together 1 tablespoon of the oil with the balsamic vinegar and maple syrup, then pour over the parsnips and toss to coat. Transfer to a baking tray and sprinkle with some salt. Bake in the preheated oven for 25 minutes, until tender and golden around the edges.

Put the roast parsnips in a high-speed blender with the chickpeas, lemon juice, the remaining 2 tablespoons of olive oil and the tahini and blend on high until smooth. Spoon into a clean jar and drizzle a little olive oil on top. Store in the fridge for up to six days.

To prepare the miso mushrooms, heat the oil in a frying pan over a high heat. Add the mushrooms and cook for 2 minutes. In a separate small bowl whisk together the tamari, maple syrup and miso, then add to the pan, stirring to coat the mushrooms. Cook for 2 minutes more.

To serve, spread the toast thickly with the roast parsnip hummus, then pile on the miso mushrooms and garnish with chopped fresh herbs.

LUNCH

Breaking up the day

Lunch is usually on the go for me. Occasionally I'll be at home, but even then it's often rushed. But I do prioritise one thing at lunchtime – I do nothing but eat. The phone is put away (after I get a quick snap for Instagram, of course), the laptop is shut and I always sit down. I used to be awful about eating on the go – I'd literally be walking somewhere while eating – or grabbing mouthfuls in between writing emails.

We all need a break, so take that 15 or 20 minutes to yourself to enjoy some good, easy food. This chapter is based around my favourite lunchbox dishes or bowls. My go-to soup has to be the courgette, chickpea and pea soup, it's so simple and really satisfying. My favourite salad is called just that on page 83, so no surprise there, and I could have the curried chickpea sliders every day.

Serves 4

TOMATO LENTIL SOUP

This soup is perfect for prepping ahead of time. I love this just as it is, but sometimes I add some tasty tofu bites (page 188) for a little more texture.

1 tbsp olive oil

1 brown onion, peeled and finely diced

1 x 400g tin of chopped tomatoes

100g red split lentils, rinsed

2 tsp curry paste

400ml vegetable stock

1 x 400ml tin of coconut milk (or 150ml more vegetable stock)

juice of ½ a lemon

To garnish:

chopped fresh flat-leaf parsley

Heat the oil in a large saucepan over a medium heat. Add the onion and cook for 4 to 5 minutes with the lid on to allow the onion to sweat. Once the onion is tender, add the tomatoes, lentils, curry paste and stock. The pan should be at a steady simmer within a few minutes. Put the lid back on and cook for 12 minutes, until the lentils are tender.

Add the coconut milk (or extra stock) along with the lemon juice, then blend until smooth with a hand-held blender.

To serve, ladle into warmed bowls and garnish with chopped fresh parsley.

CHICKPEA NOODLE SOUP

A vegan take on one of the most comforting bowls for your time
of need! I was miserably sick over Christmas and was craving a
good old-fashioned noodle soup and this version did the job.

1 tbsp oil

1 brown onion, peeled
   and finely diced

2 carrots, peeled and
   diced into small chunks

2 celery sticks,
   finely chopped

3 garlic cloves, peeled
   and crushed

1 x 2.5cm piece of fresh
   ginger, peeled and grated

2 sprigs of fresh thyme

1 tbsp dried parsley

2½ litres vegetable stock

1 x 400g tin of chickpeas,
   drained and rinsed

150g rice noodles

3 tbsp tamari or soy sauce

sea salt and freshly ground
   black pepper

2 tbsp sriracha hot sauce
   (optional)

To garnish:

fresh coriander leaves

fresh flat-leaf parsley leaves

Heat the oil in a large saucepan over a low-medium heat.
Add the onion, carrots and celery and cook for 4 to 5
minutes with the lid on to allow the veg to sweat. Once
the veg are tender, toss in the garlic and ginger and cook
for 1 minute.

Add the herbs and stock. Bring to the boil, then reduce
the heat to a steady simmer and cook for 25 minutes.

Tip in the chickpeas, rice noodles and tamari or soy sauce.
Stir to combine, then cover the pan with a lid and continue
to simmer for a couple of minutes, until the rice noodles
are cooked.

Season well with salt and pepper, then ladle into warmed
bowls, drizzle with sriracha hot sauce (if using) and scatter
with the fresh herbs.

POTATO LEEK SOUP

This one is for my sister, who is forever asking me to make her potato leek soup. In fairness, she's a whizz in the kitchen too. I'd better watch out!

1 tbsp olive oil

2 large leeks, white parts only, washed, trimmed and sliced

2 garlic cloves, peeled and crushed

1 bunch of fresh parsley, chopped, plus extra to garnish

2 tbsp snipped fresh chives, plus extra to garnish

1 tsp dried parsley

600g potatoes (about 3), peeled and diced

1 litre vegetable stock

200ml soy, unsweetened almond or coconut milk

Heat the oil in a large saucepan over a medium–high heat. Add the leeks, garlic and herbs and cook for 2 to 3 minutes, until softened. Toss in the diced potatoes and pour over the stock. Place a lid on the pan and simmer for 15 minutes, until the potatoes are tender.

Pour in the milk and stir to combine, then blend with a hand-held blender until smooth.

To serve, ladle the soup into warmed bowls and garnish with fresh herbs.

TOFU LAKSA

I've become a little obsessed with Indonesian cooking since my travels there. After I returned I must have had laksa every night for a month, so this recipe has been perfected to make every spoonful feel like you're somewhere exotic, living your best life! This recipe makes about 4 tablespoons of curry paste, but you could use the same amount of a shop-bought curry paste instead.

250g rice noodles

1 tbsp oil

400g tofu, diced

80ml water

600g mushrooms, sliced

2 heads of bok choy, diced (or use spinach)

2½ litres vegetable stock

1 x 400ml tin of full-fat coconut milk

juice of 2 limes

2½ tbsp tamari or soy sauce

2½ tbsp maple syrup

For the paste:

2 shallots, finely chopped

4 garlic cloves, crushed

2 fresh chillies, deseeded and finely chopped

1 x 5cm piece of fresh ginger, peeled and grated

3 tbsp oil

1 tbsp ground cumin

1 tbsp ground coriander

2 tsp paprika

1 tsp ground turmeric

To garnish:

chopped fresh coriander

Mix all the paste ingredients together in a small bowl, then set aside (or use 4 tablespoons of a shop-bought curry paste instead).

Cook the rice noodles according to the packet instructions. Drain and set aside.

Heat the oil in a frying pan over a high heat. Add the tofu and cook until the edges turn golden. Remove from the pan and set aside.

Set a large saucepan over a medium–high heat. Add the curry paste and stir for 30 seconds before adding the water. Toss in the mushrooms and the bok choy. Cook for 2 minutes, stirring to coat the veg in the paste. Pour in the stock and bring to the boil for 1 minute before turning the heat down a little to a steady simmer for 15 minutes.

Stir in the tofu and cooked rice noodles along with the coconut milk, lime juice, tamari or soy sauce and maple syrup and cook for 1 to 2 minutes, until heated through.

To serve, ladle the soup into warmed bowls and garnish with fresh coriander.

COURGETTE, CHICKPEA AND PEA SOUP

All my favourite things loaded into one bowl! This soup is so smooth, creamy and, most importantly, fast – perfect for those times you get in after a cold day out.

2 tbsp olive oil

2 large courgettes, thinly sliced

800ml hot vegetable stock

1 x 400g tin of chickpeas, drained and rinsed, with a few reserved as garnish

200g frozen peas, with a few defrosted peas reserved as garnish

4 tbsp vegan basil pesto (page 86), plus extra to garnish

sea salt and freshly ground black pepper

Heat the oil in a large saucepan over a high heat. Add the courgettes and cook for 4 to 5 minutes, until softened. Add the stock and simmer for 8 to 10 minutes, until the courgettes are fully cooked. Stir in the chickpeas, frozen peas and pesto and cook for 1 minute. Blend until smooth with a hand-held blender and season to taste.

To serve, ladle the soup into warmed bowls and garnish with extra pesto and the reserved chickpeas and peas.

Serves 4

CHUNKY LENTIL AND SPINACH SOUP

Don't get me wrong, I love a smooth soup, but sometimes a soup with bite feels far more satisfying. This is the perfect meal to cure those January blues.

1 tbsp olive oil

2 carrots, peeled and diced into small cubes

2 celery sticks, chopped

1 large potato or sweet potato (about 200g), peeled and diced into small cubes

2 garlic cloves, peeled and crushed

1 tbsp ground cumin

2 tsp dried oregano

1 tsp ground turmeric

1 tsp paprika

1½ litres vegetable stock

1 x 400g tin of green or brown lentils, drained and rinsed

200g spinach, chopped

Heat the oil in a large saucepan over a medium-high heat. Add the carrots, celery and potato and cook for a few minutes, until the veg have started to soften. Add the garlic, herbs and spices and cook for 1 minute. Add the stock and bring to the boil. Lower the heat to a steady simmer and cook for 10 to 12 minutes, until the veg are tender.

Stir in the lentils and spinach and cook for 1 minute, until the lentils have warmed through and the spinach has wilted down. Now it's ready to serve!

Serves 2

SIMPLE CREAMY MUSHROOM SOUP

The title says it all. Whether you want to serve this smooth or with more texture, I guarantee you'll be making this more than once.

1 tbsp olive oil

1 brown onion, peeled and diced

4 large garlic cloves, peeled and crushed

2 sprigs of fresh thyme, leaves stripped and chopped, plus extra for garnish

500g mushrooms, sliced

350ml vegetable stock

1 x 400ml tin of full-fat coconut milk

To serve:

quinoa bread (page 197)

Heat the oil in a large saucepan over a medium heat. Add the onion and cook for 3 to 4 minutes, until soft (this will depend on how small you cut the onion). Add the garlic and thyme and cook for 1 minute.

Add the mushrooms and cook for 8 minutes, until the mushrooms are cooked through. Add the vegetable stock and bring to the boil before removing the pan from the heat and stirring in the coconut milk. You can blend the soup if you like it smooth or leave it as it is if you want it chunky.

Ladle the soup into warmed bowls and garnish with fresh thyme leaves. Serve with quinoa bread on the side.

TORTILLA SALAD

Even if you think you don't like salads, you'll love this. It's got an irresistible combo of crunch and a creamy dressing, perfect for a summer day.

2 wraps, cut into triangles

2 ripe beef tomatoes, diced into small cubes

½ a red onion, peeled and finely diced

½ a head of iceberg lettuce, shredded

1 x 200g tin of sweetcorn, drained and rinsed

1 x 400g tin of black beans, drained and rinsed

For the dressing:

60g cashews

juice of 2 limes

100ml water

1 tbsp tomato purée

2 tsp maple syrup

½ tsp paprika

½ tsp onion powder (optional)

To garnish:

fresh coriander leaves

Preheat the oven to 180°C.

Start by putting the wraps on a large baking tray in a single layer and toasting in the preheated oven for 10 to 12 minutes, until golden and crisp.

Meanwhile, put the tomatoes, red onion, lettuce, sweetcorn and black beans in a large bowl and toss to combine.

To make the dressing, put all the ingredients in a blender and blitz until smooth.

To serve, put the tortilla 'chips' on the base of a serving platter. Scatter the salad over the 'chips', then drizzle everything with the dressing and garnish with fresh coriander leaves.

MY FAVOURITE SALAD

I could eat this all day. You know when you make a big batch of something and you get sick of whatever it is you've made by day three? Well, believe me, you won't get tired of this – it's got so much flavour and bite!

200g kale, leaves stripped from the stems and shredded

1 x 400g tin of cannellini beans, drained and rinsed

400g cooked quinoa

80g whole almonds, roasted

40g pumpkin seeds, roasted

2 ripe avocados, peeled, stoned and sliced

2 large ripe tomatoes, diced

For the vinaigrette:

juice of 2 limes

3 tbsp olive oil

1½ tbsp maple syrup

1 tbsp apple cider vinegar

To make the vinaigrette, whisk together all the ingredients.

Pop the kale into a large bowl and drizzle over the vinaigrette. Use your hands to toss the kale in the vinaigrette, making sure it's all coated.

To serve, arrange all the ingredients in separate neat piles in the individual serving bowls. However, if you're prepping this ahead of time, keep all the parts separate until the morning, then combine in a lunchbox and bring the dressing in a separate jar.

Serves 4

VEGGIE BEAN BOWL

I love this for lunch on the go. It's so easy to load into a lunchbox.
When I have it with me on a day out, I count down the minutes until lunch.

1 head of broccoli, broken into florets

1 head of cauliflower, broken into florets

2 large carrots, peeled and diced very small

2 tbsp olive oil

pinch of sea salt

1 tsp freshly ground black pepper

2 x 400g tins of mixed beans, drained and rinsed

4 tbsp vegan basil pesto (page 86)

To garnish:

chopped fresh herbs, such as chives or flat-leaf parsley

To serve:

lemon wedges

Preheat the oven to 180°C.

Put the broccoli, cauliflower and carrots on a large baking tray. Drizzle with the olive oil and season with the salt and pepper.

Bake in the preheated oven for 25 minutes. The carrots should be tender and the broccoli and cauliflower lightly browned.

Tip the veg into a large bowl. Add the beans and pesto and stir to combine.

Transfer to a large serving bowl or lunchbox. Garnish with the fresh herbs and serve with lemon wedges on the side.

PEA PESTO PASTA

Simple and satisfying, but make sure you portion it out – it's
so comforting, I could eat this entire batch in one go!

160g pasta

100g frozen garden
peas, defrosted

10 to 12 semi sun-dried
tomatoes, chopped

handful of hemp seeds,
crushed

For the pesto:

3 handfuls of fresh basil
leaves (remove the stalks)

100g frozen garden
peas, defrosted

100g toasted almonds

3 garlic cloves, crushed

juice of ½ a lemon

6 tbsp olive oil

3 to 4 tbsp nutritional yeast

Cook the pasta according to the packet instructions.
Drain well.

Meanwhile, defrost the frozen peas in a heatproof bowl
of hot water for 4 to 5 minutes, then drain well.

To make the pesto, blend all the ingredients until mostly
smooth – there should still be some almond chunks.

Put the drained pasta back in the pan. Add 2 to 4 tablespoons
of pesto and stir to coat all the pasta with the sauce.

Divide the pasta between two serving bowls, then divide
the peas and chopped sun-dried tomatoes between them.
Sprinkle with hemp seeds and serve straight away.

BAKED CITRUS TOFU SALAD

This light, zingy salad is perfect for BBQ season and will please everyone, even the meat eaters. You can get packets of ready-cooked quinoa and frozen cauliflower rice in most supermarkets now, which makes this salad even quicker and easier to throw together.

3 garlic cloves, peeled and crushed

juice of 1 lemon

2 tbsp olive oil, plus extra for roasting

1 tbsp dried mixed herbs

pinch of sea salt

1 x 400g block of tofu, cut into cubes

1 x 400g tin of chickpeas, drained and rinsed

200g cooked quinoa or cauliflower rice

1 courgette, thinly sliced lengthways

1 ripe avocado, peeled, stoned and diced

For the dressing:

handful of fresh flat-leaf parsley, finely chopped

6 fresh mint leaves, finely chopped

juice of ½ an orange

2 tbsp olive oil

1 tbsp maple syrup

1 tbsp balsamic vinegar

2 tsp wholegrain mustard

pinch of sea salt

Preheat the oven to 180°C.

Mix together the garlic, lemon juice, the 2 tablespoons of oil, mixed herbs and salt in a bowl. Add the tofu cubes and chickpeas and gently toss to coat. Spread out on a baking tray and bake in the preheated oven for 20 minutes, until the tofu is golden around the edges and the chickpeas are nicely browned.

Place the courgette slices on a separate baking tray and drizzle with a little oil. Roast in the oven for 8 to 10 minutes, until tender.

To make the dressing, whisk together all the ingredients in a bowl.

To assemble the salad, put all the salad ingredients in a large bowl and toss gently to combine. Divide between two serving bowls and drizzle over the dressing.

Serves 2

CURRIED CHICKPEA SLIDERS

Chickpeas in a sambo? Yes, really! Don't dis it until you
try it, and trust me on the curry flavour.

*1 x 400g tin of chickpeas,
    drained and rinsed*

30g raisins

*3 tbsp vegan mayo
    (see the potato salad
    recipe on page 156)*

*2 tbsp chopped fresh
    flat-leaf parsley*

1 tbsp curry powder

pinch of sea salt

4 slices of rye bread

*2 tbsp sauerkraut (the
    pink variety adds a
    fun pop of colour)*

chopped fresh herbs

baby salad leaves

Put the chickpeas in a bowl and mash them with a fork.
You don't want them to be too smooth – some pieces
should still be visible. Stir in the raisins, vegan mayo,
parsley, curry powder and salt.

Divide between two slices of rye bread and top with
the sauerkraut, fresh herbs and baby salad leaves before
sandwiching together with the remaining bread.

QUINOA FALAFEL

I love a good falafel, and these are nice and crisp even without deep-frying.
Prep these in advance for tasty bites, wraps or Buddha bowls all week long.

1 x 400g tin of chickpeas,
  drained and rinsed
4 tbsp quinoa
50g fresh parsley leaves
1 large garlic clove, peeled
juice of ½ a lemon
1 tbsp ground cumin
1 tsp ground coriander
1 tsp paprika
sea salt and freshly ground
  black pepper
1 to 2 tbsp olive oil

For the dressing:
juice of ½ a lemon
4 tbsp tahini
1 tbsp apple cider vinegar
1 tbsp maple syrup
1 tbsp water
pinch of sea salt

To serve:
3 wraps
beetroot hummus
sauerkraut
baby kale
sliced avocado
quartered cherry tomatoes
black sesame seeds
chopped fresh herbs

Preheat the oven to 190°C. Line a baking tray with non-stick baking paper.

Pat the chickpeas dry with some kitchen paper. Set aside.

Put the uncooked quinoa in a high-speed blender and blitz to a flour texture. Tip into a small bowl and set aside.

Blend the parsley, garlic, lemon juice and spices in a food processor until broken down. Add the chickpeas and seasoning to the food processor and pulse to combine. Depending on the strength of your food processor, pulse for 3 to 4 minutes, until the chickpeas have almost completely broken down. It will look like a dry paste with small bits of chickpeas still visible. You might need to scrape down the sides of the bowl a few times to get it to mix fully. Stir in the quinoa flour using a spoon.

Pinch off sections of the mix and roll into golf ball-sized balls (you should aim to make nine), then place on the lined baking tray. Press down the balls to flatten then slightly – they should be about 1.5cm high.

Drizzle with the oil, then bake in the preheated oven for 25 minutes, until golden and crisp on the edges.

Meanwhile, to make the dressing, whisk together all the ingredients.

To serve, put a few falafel in a wrap with some beetroot hummus, sauerkraut, baby kale, avocado and tomatoes, then scatter over some black sesame seeds and chopped fresh herbs. Drizzle with the dressing, wrap it up tightly and tuck in.

Serves 4

LUNCHTIME BURRITOS

This vegan mince started off as a total mistake. I was recipe testing and thought I had created a dud. It was sitting in the fridge for a few days because I hate food waste, so I was determined to use it for something. I woke up one morning starving after a few days in London with no food prep done. I decided to crumble up the mix and fry it along with some spinach as a burrito filling – and it was great! Not to blow my own trumpet, but it's been the perfect replacement for that 'mincey' taste.

2 tbsp oil

½ a red onion, peeled and grated

1 small garlic clove, peeled and crushed

1½ tsp allspice

1 tsp paprika

1 x 400g tin of kidney beans, drained and rinsed

40g porridge oats

1½ tbsp tamari or soy sauce

1 tbsp vegan Worcestershire sauce

sea salt and freshly ground black pepper

Fillings:

100g sweet potato, peeled and chopped into cubes

4 wraps

½ a head of green cabbage, shredded

1 ripe avocado, peeled, stoned and sliced

coconut yogurt

drizzle of sriracha hot sauce (optional)

First steam the sweet potato for the filling. An easy way to steam sweet potatoes is to add them to a small microwave-safe bowl with a little water (pour in enough water to cover the potatoes by 5cm to 7.5cm). Cover the bowl with a plate and microwave on full power for 4 to 5 minutes, until tender when pierced with the tip of a knife. Drain off any excess water and set aside while you make the mince.

Heat 1 tablespoon of the oil in a frying pan over a high heat. When the oil is sizzling, add the onion and fry for 30 seconds, stirring to ensure it doesn't burn. Add the garlic and spices and cook for 1 minute. Remove the pan from the heat and leave to one side for a moment.

Put the kidney beans in a blender and blitz for 20 seconds. They should be mostly broken down with some beans still visible. Scrape the beans into a medium-sized bowl. Stir in the rest of the ingredients, including the onion mix, and combine well. You can make the 'mince' up to this point and store it in an airtight container in the fridge for up to six days or use it straight away.

Heat the remaining tablespoon of oil in a frying pan over a high heat. Break up the 'mince' into crumbs using your fingers, then add to the pan and cook for 3 minutes, stirring constantly.

To assemble the burritos, lay out the wraps and add some shredded cabbage, followed by some sweet potato, avocado and 'mince', then drizzle with a little coconut yogurt and sriracha (if using). Wrap up tightly, cut in half on the diagonal and enjoy now or later.

DINNER

And how many hours until...?

I take dinnertime seriously. I pretty much start thinking about what I'm going to cook for dinner as soon as I finish breakfast. Saying that, though, my life has got a lot busier and that's why these meals are easy. I want a delicious meal, but not at the cost of too much effort, a messy kitchen and loads of ingredients I have to track down. I wanted this chapter to be for the everyday cook who, like me, leads a busy life. I usually have dinner with my boyfriend, discussing our day and catching up before we both sign off from our emails and sit down to watch our latest Netflix infatuation.

SIMPLE LASAGNE

Comfort food at its best, this lighter lasagne, with a creamy tofu base and juicy courgettes, is just as good as a more traditional version. People won't believe you when you tell them how easy it is to make.

For the lasagne sheets:

2 large courgettes

For the veggie layer:

1 tbsp oil

1 garlic clove, peeled and finely chopped

1 x 400g tin of green or brown lentils, drained and rinsed

1 tbsp dried basil

1 jar of shop-bought marinara sauce

12 cherry tomatoes, halved

For the tofu béchamel:

400g firm tofu

juice of ½ a lemon

4 tbsp nutritional yeast

4 tbsp vegan basil pesto (page 86)

Preheat the oven to 190°C.

Start by prepping your courgettes. Cut both the ends off, then peel lengthways into strips with a mandolin (be careful!) or a regular peeler. You may have some courgette left over because you couldn't peel off any more strips, which is fine. Set aside.

For the veggie layer, heat the oil in a saucepan over a medium–high heat. Add the garlic and stir for a moment to let it brown a little. Add the lentils and dried basil and cook for 1 minute. Pour in the marinara sauce and bring to the boil, then lower the heat and simmer for 5 minutes. Remove from the heat and set aside.

To make the béchamel, put all the ingredients in a blender and blitz into a smooth, thick sauce.

To assemble, spread half of the lentil mix over the base of an ovenproof pie dish. Add a layer of courgette slices on top (aim to use half the slices), followed by half of the béchamel sauce. Add the rest of the lentils and another layer of courgettes, followed by the last of the béchamel. Scatter over the cherry tomatoes.

Bake in the preheated oven for 35 minutes, until the lasagne is bubbling. Remove from the oven and let the lasagne stand for 10 to 15 minutes before cutting.

SWEET POTATO PIZZA

This thin, crisp pizza base with a hint of sweetness goes great with any toppings. I love it with pesto, then loaded up with ricotta, red onion and crispy kale, but you can use whatever toppings you like or whatever you have in your kitchen. The base also freezes well, so I always make a few at a time for an even faster Friday night dinner.

For the base:

400g sweet potato, peeled and diced

200g oats (porridge, rolled or jumbo oats will all work)

2 tbsp dried oregano

2 tbsp olive oil, plus extra for greasing

For the toppings:

vegan basil pesto (page 86)

cashew cheese (page 186)

sweet red onion (page 62)

crispy kale

pine nuts

Preheat the oven to 200°C. Grease two pizza pans or large baking trays with a little oil.

Steam the sweet potato on the hob or in the microwave (see page 94) until tender.

Meanwhile, blitz the oats to a flour consistency in your blender, then tip into a medium-sized bowl.

Put the steamed sweet potato in the blender along with the oregano and olive oil and blend until smooth. Pour into the bowl with the oat flour and use a spoon to combine into a dough.

Split the dough in half. Working with one half at a time, tip the dough out onto a clean surface (you shouldn't need any extra flour for dusting and rolling) and roll it out nice and thin into a 20cm circle. Repeat with the other half.

Use a spatula to lift the dough onto the greased pizza pans or trays. Bake in the preheated oven for 25 minutes.

Remove from the oven and flip the base over, then add your toppings. Place the pizza back in the oven for 5 to 8 minutes, depending on your toppings. Remove from the oven and allow to stand for 1 minute before cutting into slices.

SWEET AND SOUR CHICKPEAS

Sweet and sour was a favourite of ours growing up – when Mum was away, Dad would let us get a takeaway (sorry, Dad, I've ruined the secret!). But you don't need to go to the takeaway to get that tangy, sweet taste when you can make this in minutes.

1 tbsp oil

1 large or 2 small garlic cloves, peeled and finely chopped

1 x 4cm piece of fresh ginger, peeled and grated

1 red pepper, deseeded and sliced

1 yellow pepper, deseeded and sliced

1 green pepper, deseeded and sliced

2 x 400g tins of chickpeas, drained and rinsed (or try the crispy tofu from the katsu curry recipe on page 109)

2 tbsp tamari or soy sauce

2 tbsp maple syrup

To serve:

your favourite noodles or boiled basmati rice

lime wedges

Heat the oil in a large frying pan over a high heat. Add the garlic and ginger and cook for 30 seconds. Toss in the peppers and cook for 6 to 7 minutes, stirring occasionally, until softened.

Stir in the chickpeas, tamari or soy sauce and the maple syrup and cook for a few minutes more to heat through.

Divide between two serving bowls and serve with noodles or rice and lime wedges for squeezing over.

Serves 4

QUICK VEGGIE CURRY

My friends call me 'Three Curries' Purcell for my overeager consumption of curry on a regular basis. It's probably my favourite food, and why not? It's so easy and tasty!

1 tbsp oil or 50ml water

1 large onion, peeled and finely diced

1 garlic clove, peeled and finely diced

2 tbsp curry powder

1 tbsp tomato purée

2 carrots, peeled and diced

1 small head of broccoli, broken into small florets

400g sweet potato (about 2 small potatoes), peeled and diced into small chunks

120g red split lentils, rinsed (or 1 x 400g tin, drained and rinsed)

600ml vegetable stock (if using tinned lentils, use only 250ml stock)

100g spinach leaves, chopped

1 x 400ml tin of coconut milk

1½ tbsp tamari or soy sauce

To garnish:

fresh coriander leaves

toasted sesame seeds

To serve:

boiled basmati rice

Heat the oil or water in a large saucepan over a high heat. Toss in the onion and cook for 1 to 2 minutes, stirring constantly to ensure it doesn't burn. Once the onion is lightly coloured, add the garlic along with the curry powder and cook for 1 minute. Add the tomato purée and cook for 1 minute more.

Add the carrots, broccoli, sweet potatoes and lentils, then pour in the vegetable stock. Bring to the boil, then lower the heat to a steady simmer and cook, covered with a lid, for 15 minutes.

Once the veg are tender, stir in the chopped spinach along with the coconut milk and tamari or soy sauce. Cook for 1 minute to warm through.

To serve, ladle the curry into warmed bowls and garnish with fresh coriander leaves and toasted sesame seeds. Serve with basmati rice.

Serves 2

GREEN CURRY

You didn't think I would have only one curry in my book, did you? I have to have tons of variations for whatever curry mood you or I may find ourselves in! This is a light and mild curry for a quick and easy dinner to warm you up.

1 tbsp oil or 50ml water

2 garlic cloves, peeled and finely chopped

1 x 2.5cm piece of fresh ginger, peeled and grated

1 small head of broccoli, broken into florets

1 red pepper, deseeded and diced into small cubes

½ an aubergine, diced into small cubes

350ml vegetable stock

2 tbsp shop-bought green curry paste

400g tofu, diced, or 1 x 400g tin of jackfruit, drained and diced

1 x 400ml tin of coconut milk

To serve:
boiled basmati rice

Heat the oil or water in a large saucepan over a medium-high heat. Add the garlic and ginger and cook for 1 minute. Add the broccoli, red pepper, aubergine, stock and green curry paste. Bring to the boil, then reduce the heat to a steady simmer for 12 minutes, until the veggies are tender.

Lower the heat a little, then stir in the tofu or jackfruit and the coconut milk. Cook for 1 or 2 minutes more to warm through, then divide between two warmed bowls and serve with basmati rice.

KATSU CURRY

This is the most requested dinner recipe from you guys over on social media. This is really easy to whip up – even the coated tofu, I promise! The curry sauce can also be used for so many other things, like drizzling over chips (I love a curry chip) or as a dip with vegetables. It's thick, creamy and mild, so if you love your spice, like me, go on and add a little chilli.

100ml unsweetened almond milk

2 tbsp chickpea flour

1 tbsp tamari or soy sauce

1 tbsp tomato purée

½ tbsp maple syrup

100g ground almonds, ground uncooked quinoa or breadcrumbs

400g firm tofu

For the katsu curry sauce:

350ml unsweetened almond milk

3 tbsp smooth almond butter

1½ tbsp curry powder

1 tbsp tomato purée

1 tbsp nutritional yeast (optional)

1 tsp tamari or soy sauce (optional)

To serve:

boiled wild rice

Preheat the oven to 190°C.

Combine the almond milk, chickpea flour, tamari or soy sauce, tomato purée and maple syrup in a shallow bowl. Put the ground almonds, ground quinoa or breadcrumbs in a second shallow bowl beside the chickpea batter.

Line a baking tray with non-stick baking paper and set it next to the bowl of ground almonds.

Cut the tofu into slices about 1cm thick. Working with one slice at a time, dip one piece of tofu into the chickpea batter, gently shaking off any excess, then coat in the ground almonds, quinoa or breadcrumbs, again shaking off any excess. Put each coated slice on the lined baking tray. Repeat until all the tofu is coated. Bake the tofu in the preheated oven for 35 minutes.

Meanwhile, to make the curry sauce, pour the almond milk into a small saucepan and bring to a gentle simmer. Add the almond butter, curry powder and tomato purée, stirring constantly to ensure the sauce isn't sticking to the bottom of the pan. You may need to use a balloon whisk here to stop the almond butter from clumping. The sauce will thicken up, which is good – you want it to be as thick and smooth as a regular curry sauce. Remove from the heat, then stir in the nutritional yeast and tamari or soy sauce (if using).

To serve, do you want to dunk the crispy tofu in the sauce or drizzle it over? It's up to you! Either way, serve with boiled wild rice.

CHICKPEA AND COURGETTE CURRY

This really is a curry in a hurry. Wake up your sinuses and get your plates ready!

50ml water

1 onion, peeled and diced very finely

2 garlic cloves, peeled and grated

1 x 5cm piece of fresh ginger, peeled and grated

3 tbsp shop-bought curry paste (I use red)

2 courgettes, diced into small chunks

1 x 400g tin of chickpeas, drained and rinsed

1 x 400g tin of chopped tomatoes

1 x 400ml tin of coconut milk

150g baby spinach, chopped

juice of 1 lime

1 tbsp tamari or soy sauce

To serve:

boiled basmati rice

Heat the water in a large deep saucepan over a high heat. Add the onion and let it sizzle for 1 minute to soften. Toss in the garlic, ginger and curry paste and cook for 1 minute, stirring constantly.

Add the courgettes, chickpeas, tomatoes and coconut milk and stir to combine everything. Bring to the boil, then lower the heat and let it simmer for 5 minutes.

Stir in the spinach, lime juice and the tamari or soy sauce and cook for 1 minute before removing from the heat and serving with boiled basmati rice.

POT NOODLE

One-pot wonder to the rescue! This dinner is perfect for busy days.
I've given the option to add peanut butter; you don't have to use it,
but for a creamier, nuttier pot noodle, you know what to do.

1 tbsp oil

1 x 5cm piece of fresh ginger,
    peeled and grated

250g tofu, diced into cubes

3 tbsp curry paste (I use red)

1 litre vegetable stock

250g rice noodles

1 sweet potato (250g),
    peeled and diced
    into cubes

1 large courgette, diced

200g broccoli stems

1 x 400ml tin of coconut
    milk

juice of 1 lime

1½ tbsp tamari or soy sauce

3 tbsp peanut butter
    (optional)

2 tbsp sriracha hot sauce
    (optional)

To garnish:

handful of spring onions,
    thinly sliced

fresh coriander leaves

diced fresh red chilli

Heat the oil in a large saucepan over a high heat. Add the ginger and cook for 40 seconds, until lightly coloured. Toss in the tofu cubes and cook for 1 minute, stirring gently. Add the curry paste and 100ml of the stock and cook for 1 minute.

Add the noodles, sweet potato, courgette, broccoli and the rest of the stock and bring to the boil. Put the lid on, then reduce the heat a little and let it simmer for 5 minutes, until the broccoli and noodles are tender.

Remove from the heat and stir in the coconut milk, lime juice and tamari or soy sauce along with the peanut butter and hot sauce (if using).

Ladle into warmed bowls and garnish each one with some spring onions, fresh coriander leaves and chilli. Or if you want to make this ahead, it will keep for up to three days in the fridge.

CREAMY MUSHROOM AND CAULIFLOWER PASTA

Fool everyone with this creamy vegan sauce that's rich and flavoursome. This sauce is also really good as a béchamel for lasagne or drizzled over vegetables.

500g tagliatelle

1 tbsp oil

200g mushrooms of choice, sliced

2 garlic cloves, peeled and finely chopped

1 tbsp dried parsley

For the sauce:

1 small head of cauliflower, broken into small florets

100g raw cashews

200ml vegetable stock

4 tbsp nutritional yeast

pinch of sea salt

½ tsp freshly ground black pepper

To garnish:

chopped fresh flat-leaf parsley

chopped fresh thyme

Start making the sauce by steaming the cauliflower on the hob for 20 minutes, until tender. Or you can steam it in the microwave by placing the florets in a microwave-safe bowl and pouring over enough water to cover the florets by 5cm to 7.5cm of water. Cover the bowl with a plate and cook on high for 2 to 3 minutes, until tender.

Meanwhile, bring a large saucepan of salted water to the boil and cook the pasta according to the packet instructions. Drain well.

Tip the steamed cauliflower into a blender along with the cashews, stock, nutritional yeast and salt and pepper. Blend on high until the sauce is smooth.

Using the same pan that you cooked the pasta in, heat the oil over a high heat. Add the mushrooms, garlic and parsley and cook for 2 to 3 minutes, until tender.

Add the cooked pasta and cauliflower sauce and stir to combine. Garnish with chopped fresh parsley and thyme and serve immediately or allow to cool fully before storing in a lunchbox in the fridge for up to three days.

VEGAN MEATBALLS

These 'meatballs' look just like the real deal but taste even better. They're perfect in a ragù sauce, loaded into a wrap or just as a savoury snack.

1 x 400g tin of kidney beans, drained and rinsed

80g walnuts

80g oats (porridge, rolled or jumbo oats will all work)

2 tbsp vegan red pesto or basil pesto (page 86)

1 tbsp tamari or soy sauce

To serve:

sweet potato and lentil mash (page 150)

Preheat the oven to 200°C. Line a baking tray with non-stick baking paper.

Put all the ingredients in a blender or food processor and blend to form a thick, heavy dough. Pinch off sections of the dough and roll into balls. Place on the lined baking tray as you go.

Bake in the preheated oven for 25 minutes. (Alternatively, you can pan-fry these in a little oil for 5 to 6 minutes.) Eat these however you like, but I like to serve them with sweet potato and lentil mash.

SIMPLE BOLOGNESE SAUCE

You can never go wrong with this dish and the best part is that it takes only minutes to cook. I like to prep the veggies ahead of time and stash them in the fridge so that when I get in the door, I know that dinner is only 15 minutes away from being on the table.

1 small brown onion, peeled and roughly chopped

3 large carrots, peeled and roughly chopped

2 celery sticks, roughly chopped

400g button mushrooms, stems removed

1 tbsp oil or 50ml water

4 garlic cloves, peeled and crushed

2 sprigs of fresh rosemary, needles stripped and finely chopped

1 tbsp dried oregano

1½ tsp dried thyme

1 tsp chilli flakes

1 x 400g tin of chopped tomatoes

2½ tbsp balsamic vinegar

1 tbsp tomato purée

1 x 400g tin of green or brown lentils, drained and rinsed

sea salt and freshly ground black pepper

To serve:

spaghetti or veggie noodles

Put the onion in a blender or food processor and blitz into tiny pieces. Scrape out into a bowl, then do the same with the carrots, celery and mushrooms, keeping them in a separate bowl from the onion.

Heat the oil or water in a large saucepan over a medium heat. Add the onion, then put on the lid and sweat the onion for 4 to 5 minutes, until softened but not coloured. Add the garlic, rosemary, oregano, thyme and chilli flakes and cook for 30 seconds before tossing in the carrots, celery and mushrooms and cooking for a few minutes more, until softened.

Add the tomatoes, balsamic vinegar and tomato purée. Bring to a steady simmer and cook for 5 minutes. Add the lentils and seasoning and cook for a few minutes more, until the lentils are warmed through.

Serve with spaghetti or veggie noodles.

Serves 4 to 6

JACKFRUIT STEW

If you haven't cooked with jackfruit before, don't worry, it's not difficult or scary. In fact, it's one of the easiest ingredients you can add. It doesn't have a distinctive taste, so it won't overpower any dishes.

1 tbsp oil

1 small brown onion, peeled and diced

3 garlic cloves, peeled and finely chopped

1 sprig of fresh thyme, leaves stripped and chopped

1 tbsp dried oregano

1 tbsp dried parsley

2 x 400g tins of jackfruit, drained and left whole

2 carrots, peeled and diced

2 large potatoes (500g), peeled and diced

1 red pepper, deseeded and diced

2 litres vegetable stock

2 tbsp tomato purée

1 tbsp vegan Worcestershire sauce (optional)

2 bay leaves

3 tbsp oat flour

To garnish:

chopped fresh flat-leaf parsley

Heat the oil in a large saucepan over a medium-high heat. Add the onion, then cover the pan with a lid and sweat the onion for 4 to 5 minutes, until softened but not coloured. Toss in the garlic, thyme, oregano and parsley and cook for 1 minute.

Add the jackfruit and cook for 2 minutes. Toss in the carrots, potatoes, pepper, vegetable stock, tomato purée, Worcestershire sauce (if using) and bay leaves. Bring to the boil, then lower the heat and cook for 45 minutes.

Stir in the oat flour and cook for 2 or 3 minutes to thicken the stew. Ladle into warmed bowls and garnish with a little chopped fresh parsley to serve.

SHEPHERD'S PIE

So many vegetables, all tucked into one easy dish. If you're someone who struggles to eat your veg, this would be an ideal option for you. It's comforting, satisfying and not too hard to follow – your five-a-day will be sorted!

1 tbsp olive oil

1 large brown onion, peeled and finely chopped

2 garlic cloves, peeled and crushed

1 tsp dried thyme

1 tsp paprika

½ tsp nutmeg

600g mushrooms, finely diced, or 2 x 400g tins of brown lentils, drained and rinsed

1 large carrot, peeled and finely diced into small cubes

150ml vegetable stock

3 tbsp tomato purée

200g frozen peas

2 tbsp tamari or soy sauce

For the topping:

2 potatoes (350g), peeled and diced (sweet potato works here too)

1 large head of cauliflower, broken into florets

3 tbsp nutritional yeast

1 tbsp olive oil

sea salt and freshly ground black pepper

Preheat the oven to 190°C.

Start with the topping by cooking the potatoes in a large saucepan of boiling salted water (or steam them for 15 minutes, until tender). After 5 minutes, add the cauliflower florets to cook with the potatoes. Cook for 5 to 10 minutes more, until the potatoes and cauliflower are tender, then drain well.

Heat the oil in a large pan over a medium-high heat. Add the onion and cook for 1 to 2 minutes, stirring constantly, until light golden and starting to soften. Toss in the garlic, thyme, paprika and nutmeg and cook for 2 minutes.

Add the mushrooms, carrot, stock and tomato purée and bring to the boil. Lower the heat and simmer for 8 to 10 minutes, until the carrots have softened. The cooking time will depend on how finely you diced them. Stir in the peas and the tamari or soy sauce and remove from the heat.

To make the topping, blitz the cooked potatoes and cauliflower with the nutritional yeast, olive oil and some salt and pepper in a blender or food processor until smooth.

To assemble, spoon the veggies into an ovenproof dish, then top with the smooth, creamy cauliflower mash. Even out the topping using the back of a spoon.

Bake in the preheated oven for 12 minutes, until the topping has turned golden around the edges.

NASI GORENG

I got a bit addicted to nasi goreng while I was in Bali, so it was
only right that it had a place in this book. It's become my
go-to dinner when I get hangry – it never fails to satisfy.

2 tbsp oil or 50ml water

1 x 2.5cm piece of fresh
ginger, peeled and grated

1 tbsp shop-bought curry
paste (I use yellow)

1 tsp sambal oelek or
chilli paste

2 carrots, peeled and grated
using the coarse side of
a box grater

¼ head of cabbage, shredded

250g tofu, crumbled into
pieces

2 to 3 tbsp tamari or
soy sauce

250g cooked rice

juice of 1 lime (do not
leave this out, it makes
such a difference)

Toppings:

1 or 2 spring onions,
thinly sliced

2 handfuls of roasted
peanuts, crushed

drizzle of sriracha hot sauce
(optional)

lime wedges

Heat the oil or water in a frying pan over a high heat. Add
the ginger, curry paste and the sambal or chilli paste and stir
to combine. Cook for 1 minute, then toss in the carrots and
cabbage, stirring to mix all the flavours together. Cook for
2 minutes, until the cabbage has wilted.

Stir in the crumbled tofu and the tamari or soy sauce and
cook until the tofu is just warmed through. Add the cooked
rice and cook for 2 to 3 minutes, continuing to stir to marry
all the flavours and to make sure the bottom doesn't burn.
Remove from the heat, then stir in the lime juice.

Divide the dish between two serving bowls and top with spring
onions, peanuts and a drizzle of sriracha for extra spice (if
using). Serve with lime wedges on the side for squeezing over.

ONE-POT CHILLI

You didn't think I could stop with just one one-pot wonder,
did you? I love a meal where you can just throw everything
into a pot and come back and you're ready to eat!

1 x 400g tin of black beans, drained and rinsed

1 x 400g tin of kidney beans, drained and rinsed

1 x 200g tin of sweetcorn, drained and rinsed

150g quinoa

1 small butternut squash, peeled and diced into small chunks

1 red pepper, deseeded and diced

1 yellow pepper, deseeded and diced

3 garlic cloves, peeled and crushed

400ml vegetable stock

200ml tomato passata

1 tbsp paprika

1 tbsp ground cumin

To garnish:

diced avocado

chopped fresh coriander

Put all the ingredients in a large saucepan over a high heat. Bring to the boil, then cover the pan with a lid, lower the heat a little and let it simmer for 20 minutes.

Remove the pan from the heat and let it sit for 10 minutes with the lid off before serving.

Divide the chilli between four bowls and garnish each one with some diced avocado and chopped fresh coriander.

AUBERGINE TAGINE

This all-in-one pot is such a crowd-pleaser. I love to prep this dish in advance for a big dinner party or even just for myself. With the soft aubergines, rich Middle Eastern spices and a burst of sweet fruit, it's a real taste sensation.

1 red onion, peeled and
   finely diced

2 garlic cloves, peeled
   and crushed

1 x 5cm piece of fresh ginger,
   peeled and chopped

handful of fresh coriander
   (including stems), with
   some leaves reserved
   for garnish

2 tbsp tomato purée

1 tbsp ground paprika

1 tbsp ground cumin

1 tsp ground turmeric

1 tsp ground cinnamon

2 tbsp olive oil

3 aubergines, diced into cubes

2 carrots, peeled and sliced

1 x 400g tin of chopped
   tomatoes

600ml vegetable stock

1 x 400g tin of chickpeas,
   drained and rinsed

60g dried fruit (I like to
   use apricots or sultanas)

To garnish:

pomegranate seeds

To serve:

boiled basmati rice
   or flatbreads

Put the red onion, garlic, ginger, coriander, tomato purée, spices and 1 tablespoon of the oil in a blender or food processor and blend into a thick paste.

Heat the remaining tablespoon of oil in a large saucepan over a medium-high heat. Add the paste and cook for 1 minute before adding the aubergines, carrots, tomatoes and stock. Bring to the boil, then reduce the heat to a steady simmer, cover with a lid and cook for 35 minutes.

Stir in the chickpeas and dried fruit and cook for a further 5 minutes to warm through.

To serve, divide between warmed bowls, then garnish with the reserved fresh coriander leaves and pomegranate seeds and serve with boiled basmati rice or flatbreads.

MUSHROOM AND BLACK BEAN CHILLI

This nearly didn't make it into the book – not because I questioned the recipe, but because I totally forgot I'd even made it! Just in time, my friend Sarah said, 'I hope that chilli is in the book, cause you still haven't even put it up on the blog!' It's rich in flavour, so easy to make and perfect for prepping ahead. I hope you love it just as much as Sarah does.

800g button mushrooms

1 large carrot, peeled and diced into small chunks

1 tbsp oil

2 garlic cloves, peeled and finely chopped

1 fresh red chilli, deseeded and diced

1 tbsp chilli powder

1½ tsp sweet paprika

1½ tsp ground coriander

1 tsp ground cumin

1 tsp dried thyme

1 x 400g tin of black beans or kidney beans, drained and rinsed

1 x 400g tin of chopped tomatoes

2 tbsp cacao powder

To serve:

boiled basmati rice

diced avocado

chilli flakes

Wipe the mushrooms clean, then remove and discard the stems. Put the mushroom caps and carrots in a food processor and blitz for a few seconds to dice into small pieces.

Heat the oil in a large saucepan over a medium-high heat. Toss in the garlic and chilli and cook for 1 minute. Add the mushrooms, carrots, herbs and spices and cook for 5 to 6 minutes, stirring occasionally, until the mushrooms and carrots are completely tender.

Add the beans, tomatoes and cacao powder. Bring to the boil, then reduce the heat to a gentle simmer and cook for 6 minutes more.

To serve, ladle into bowls along with some boiled basmati rice, then top with diced avocado and chilli flakes.

NO-FUSS DAHL

I crave dahl more than any other comfort dinner. I don't know what it is, but the warm, creamy, soft lentils on a bed of rice almost has the same powers as a cup of tea to help me unwind. The best part about this dish is that it's perfect for large parties or prepping ahead, it's a cheap one-pot wonder and it tastes even better the next day!

1.2 litres vegetable stock or water

1 small onion, peeled and finely diced

2 garlic cloves, peeled and finely chopped

1 x 5cm piece of fresh ginger, peeled and grated

1 fresh red chilli, deseeded and finely diced (optional)

2½ tbsp curry paste (I opt for red here, but for a milder dahl go for yellow)

1 tbsp tomato purée

500g red split lentils, rinsed

1 x 400ml tin of full-fat coconut milk

To serve:

boiled basmati rice

diced banana

non-dairy yogurt

Heat 50ml of the stock or water in a large saucepan over a medium heat. Add the onion, then put a lid on the pan and sweat the onion for 6 minutes, until tender and translucent. Add the garlic, ginger, chilli (if using), curry paste and tomato purée and cook for 1 minute. You may need to add another 50ml of stock or water here so as not to burn the onions.

Tip in the lentils and the remaining stock or water. Turn the heat up to bring to the boil, then turn the heat back down to medium and simmer for 15 minutes, stirring every so often, until the lentils have bulked up and are tender. Remove the pan from the heat and stir in the coconut milk.

Serve with boiled basmati rice. I recommend serving the dahl with some diced banana and a dollop of non-dairy yogurt on top too.

QUICK ONE-POT RICE AND VEG DISH

This dish is almost like a risotto – it's rich and creamy, but without the cream. White basmati is the only rice that will work in this short cooking time, so don't be tempted to substitute it as it gives the best result.

250g white basmati rice

1 courgette, cut into chunks

½ a head of broccoli, broken into small florets

½ a red pepper, deseeded and cut into small chunks

½ a yellow pepper, deseeded and cut into small chunks

1 litre vegetable stock

2 tbsp curry paste (any kind will work here)

200g frozen peas

3 to 4 tbsp nutritional yeast

Put the rice, courgette, broccoli, peppers, stock and curry paste in a large saucepan over a high heat. Bring to the boil, then lower the heat to keep it at a steady simmer. Cover with a lid and cook for 10 to 12 minutes, until the rice is fully cooked.

Stir in the peas and nutritional yeast and cook for 1 minute before removing from the heat, dishing up and tucking in.

Makes 4

SWEET POTATO AND BLACK BEAN BURGERS

I wanted to include one ultimate vegan burger – or should I call this a veggie disc now? Either way, this one outshines all others. After a lot of burger recipe testing and burger food babies, here it is. I hope you agree it's top notch!

150g sweet potato, peeled and cut into cubes

80g sunflower seeds, seed mix or walnuts

1 tbsp oil

1 small red onion, peeled and grated

2 garlic cloves, peeled and crushed

1 x 400g tin of black beans, drained and rinsed

2 tbsp BBQ sauce or hot sauce

1 tbsp maple syrup

2 tsp vegan Worcestershire sauce (optional)

1 tsp dried sage

1 tsp dried thyme

1 tsp paprika

To serve:

toasted burger buns

your favourite burger toppings

street corn (page 155)

potato salad (page 156)

baby salad leaves

Preheat the oven to 200°C. Line a baking tray with non-stick baking paper.

Steam the sweet potato until it's soft and cooked through. An easy way to steam sweet potatoes is in a small microwave-safe bowl with a little water (pour in enough water to cover the potatoes by 5cm to 7.5cm). Cover the bowl with a plate and microwave on full power for 4 to 5 minutes, until tender when pierced with the tip of a knife. Drain off any excess water.

Put the seeds in a blender or food processor and blitz into a flour. Tip out into a bowl and set aside.

Heat the oil in a frying pan set over a medium heat. Add the red onion and cook for 2 minutes, until softened. Add the garlic and cook for 1 minute more, then remove the pan from the heat and set aside.

Put the steamed sweet potato in the blender or food processor along with the black beans and blend to combine. Tip out into a bowl and stir in the seed 'flour', red onion and garlic, BBQ or hot sauce, maple syrup, Worcestershire sauce (if using) and spices. Pinch off sections of the mixture and roll into four even-sized balls. Gently flatten into a burger shape and place on the lined baking tray.

Bake in the preheated oven for 25 minutes, until crisp around the edges and cooked through. Serve in toasted buns with your favourite burger toppings (I like hummus, sprouts and pesto) and street corn, potato salad and baby salad leaves on the side.

Serves 4

CHICKPEA SATAY SKEWERS

The ultimate peanut lover's dinner! The nutty sauce drizzled over these soft chickpea balls is packed with so much flavour and heat.

50g oats (porridge, rolled and jumbo oats will all work)

1 x 400g tin of chickpeas, drained and rinsed

3 tbsp nutritional yeast

3 tbsp smooth peanut butter

2 tbsp hot sauce (I go for one with a medium heat)

1 tbsp maple syrup

For the satay sauce:

350ml unsweetened almond milk

3 tbsp smooth peanut butter

1½ tbsp curry powder

1 tbsp tomato purée

1 tbsp nutritional yeast (optional)

1 tsp tamari or soy sauce (optional)

Preheat the oven to 200°C.

Put the oats in a blender or food processor and blend into a flour consistency. Tip out into a bowl.

Put the chickpeas in the blender or food processor and blend into a smooth paste. Tip the paste into the bowl with the oat flour, then stir in the rest of the ingredients until well combined.

Pinch off sections of the mixture and roll into 12 balls, then thread onto four skewers. Place the skewers on a baking tray and bake in the preheated oven for 20 minutes, until crisp around the edges.

Meanwhile, to make the sauce, pour the almond milk into a small saucepan and bring to a gentle simmer. Add the peanut butter, curry powder and tomato purée, stirring constantly to ensure the sauce isn't sticking to the bottom of the pan. You may need to use a balloon whisk here to stop the peanut butter from clumping. Remove from the heat, then stir in the nutritional yeast and tamari or soy sauce (if using).

To serve, plate up the skewers and drizzle with the satay sauce.

JACKFRUIT FAJITA BOWL

This is so delicious that every time I make it at home, my boyfriend Zach thinks it's meat. It really looks like it, but it tastes way better. I love using jackfruit in recipes, as it picks up whatever flavours you pair it with. Plus it really confuses people – they're bound to ask, 'Wait, are you eating meat?!'

1 x 400g tin of jackfruit, drained

140g rice

1 x 400g tin of black beans, drained and rinsed

2 ripe tomatoes, finely diced

juice of 2 limes

1 ripe avocado, peeled, stoned and diced

1 tbsp thinly sliced jalapeño pepper (optional)

For the marinade:

2½ tbsp tamari or soy sauce

2 tbsp olive oil

2 tbsp tomato purée

1 tbsp maple syrup

1½ tsp chilli paste

1 tsp ground cumin

1 tsp smoked paprika

½ tsp chilli powder

½ tsp garlic powder

For the spicy mayo:

2 tbsp vegan mayo (see the potato salad recipe on page 156)

2 tsp sriracha hot sauce

Preheat the oven to 200°C. Line a baking tray with non-stick baking paper.

Combine all the marinade ingredients in a bowl. Use your hands to break up the jackfruit, then add to the bowl, stirring well to cover it in the marinade.

Place on the lined baking tray, then drizzle over any excess marinade from the bowl. Bake in the preheated oven for 25 minutes.

Meanwhile, cook the rice according to the packet instructions.

To make the spicy mayo, mix together the mayo and sriracha, then set aside in the fridge until you're ready to serve.

To assemble, put the black beans, tomatoes and lime juice in a bowl and stir to combine. Divide between two serving bowls, then spoon in the cooked rice and jackfruit, dividing it evenly between the bowls. Top with avocado and jalapeño (if using).

CREAMY BEAN AND CAULI BAKE

This all-in-one bake is perfect for meal prep on a Sunday night when you need something low maintenance and tasty for the busy week ahead.

1 to 2 sweet potatoes (about 350g), peeled and diced into small chunks

1 small head of cauliflower, broken into small florets

100g kale, leaves stripped from the stems and chopped

1 x 400g tin of cannellini beans, drained and rinsed

For the topping:

150g cashews

300ml vegetable stock

3 tbsp nutritional yeast

sea salt and freshly ground black pepper

Preheat the oven to 180°C.

To make the topping, put the cashews, stock, nutritional yeast and some salt and pepper in a blender or food processor and blend to combine.

Put the sweet potatoes, cauliflower, kale and beans in a large baking dish. Pour over the cashew sauce, stirring to mix everything together.

Bake in the preheated oven for 45 minutes, until the veg are tender and the top is lightly browned along the edges.

TOFU AND BROCCOLI BAKE

One of the most popular dishes in my first book, *Natural Born Feeder*, was the creamy chicken broccoli bake, so for all you fans of that recipe, here is an easy plant-based version that's not missing any of the taste.

400g broccoli florets

2 tbsp coconut oil

4 tbsp oat flour (buckwheat or chickpea flour work too)

500ml unsweetened almond milk

4 to 5 tbsp nutritional yeast

1½ tsp freshly ground black pepper

1 tsp sea salt

1 tsp tamari or soy sauce

1 tsp Dijon mustard

500g tofu, diced into small chunks

1 x 400g tin of chickpeas, drained and rinsed (optional)

125g cooked quinoa

Preheat the oven to 200°C.

Start by steaming your broccoli. You want it to be only a little tender, not mushy or falling apart. This should take 10 to 12 minutes. Set aside.

Melt the coconut oil in a medium-sized saucepan, then add the oat flour. Stir into a paste and cook for 20 to 30 seconds.

Turn the heat up and whisk in the almond milk about 100ml at a time. Stir and wait for the sauce to thicken before adding the next bit of milk. Continue until all the milk has been added – this will take about 5 minutes. The sauce should be smooth and thick, but if there are any lumps, you can use a sieve to remove them. Stir in the nutritional yeast, seasoning, tamari or soy sauce and the mustard and cook for 1 minute. Remove from the heat and stir in the steamed broccoli, tofu and chickpeas (if using).

Spoon this mix into a pie dish and evenly sprinkle over the cooked quinoa. Bake in the preheated oven for 12 minutes, until the quinoa is golden and crisp.

SIDES

A little bit on the . . .

Sides can really tart up any meal. When I was growing up, sides were a huge part of our family dinners. We would have loads of different vegetables in bowls scattered across the table. Sides don't have to be uninspiring boiled vegetables that just fill some space on your plate. They can be so much more. They can be so full of flavour that they could even be the centre of your meal. I love making lots of side dishes, so I hope you love these as much as I do. I even saved my favourites – the crunchy baked garam masala cauliflower with parsley sauce and the miso aubergines – for this book.

CRUNCHY BAKED GARAM MASALA CAULIFLOWER WITH PARSLEY SAUCE

This is one of my favourite sides – crisp, packed with flavour and easy. One great thing about this recipe is how versatile it is. For example, by breaking the cauliflower into florets you can make bites that are perfect for tacos, canapés or wraps.

5 tbsp olive oil

2 tbsp garam masala

1 tbsp curry powder

pinch of sea salt

1 head of cauliflower, cut in half down the middle

40g toasted flaked almonds

20g dried cranberries

For the parsley sauce:

120g soy or coconut yogurt

juice of 1 lemon

small handful of fresh flat-leaf parsley leaves

Preheat the oven to 200°C.

Combine the olive oil, spices and salt in a small bowl.

Place the cauliflower in a baking dish and drizzle over the spiced oil. Use your hands to rub it all over the cauliflower to cover it fully.

Bake in the preheated oven for 40 minutes, until tender and golden brown.

While the cauliflower is in the oven, blitz the yogurt, lemon juice and parsley in a blender for 30 seconds. The yogurt will turn a minty green colour and the parsley should be barely visible.

Once the cauliflower is cooked, cut each half in half again to make four wedges. Drizzle each wedge with the sauce, then scatter over the toasted flaked almonds and dried cranberries.

BBQ CAULIFLOWER BITES

If you make only one recipe from this book, this is it! These have got it all going on, with an unforgettable crunch and a sticky sauce. My mouth is watering just thinking about them!

1 small head of cauliflower, broken into florets

For the crunchy coating:

120g flour (I used a gluten-free blend, but flours such as brown rice flour and chickpea flour will work too)

1½ tbsp smoked paprika

1½ tbsp ground cumin

1 tsp onion powder

1 tsp garlic powder

220ml unsweetened almond milk

100g quinoa

For the sauce:

150ml hot sauce

2 tbsp maple syrup

To serve:

vegan cream cheese (page 63)

guacamole

Preheat the oven to 200°C. Line a baking tray with non-stick baking paper.

Combine the flour and spices in a large bowl, then whisk in the almond milk to form a smooth batter.

Put the quinoa in a blender or food processor (I use my NutriBullet) and blend to a chunky flour consistency. Tip into a separate bowl.

Using your hands, dip a cauliflower floret in the batter, making sure it's fully coated. Shake off any excess batter, then roll the floret in the quinoa flour and place on the baking tray. Repeat with all the florets.

Bake in the preheated oven for 25 minutes. They should be nice and crunchy.

While the cauliflower is baking, combine the hot sauce and maple syrup in a bowl.

Once the florets have baked for 25 minutes, remove the tray from the oven and drizzle over the sauce. Carefully mix it around using your hands (it's messy, I know!). Place the tray back in the oven and cook for a further 10 minutes.

Serve with some vegan cream cheese and guacamole or simply on their own. These are so delicious!

SWEET POTATO AND LENTIL MASH

Fan of mash? This creamy mash is soft and satisfying, perfect for serving alongside just about any kind of meal. The great thing about this side is not only the taste and comfort factor, but also the fact that you have only one pot to wash up!

1 large sweet potato, peeled and diced into chunks

100g red split lentils, rinsed

about 550ml water

1½ tbsp coconut oil

good pinch of sea salt

½ tsp freshly ground black pepper

Put the sweet potato, lentils and water in a medium-sized saucepan. Cover the pan with a lid and bring to the boil, then lower the heat slightly to a steady simmer for 12 minutes, until the sweet potato and lentils are tender. All the water should have been absorbed, but if not, let the saucepan sit with the lid off for a few minutes.

Add the coconut oil, salt and pepper, then mash using a potato masher. Serve hot.

Serves 4

MISO AUBERGINES

Okay, get ready for this! I love roasted aubergine and if this is not the best version you've ever had, then I don't know what is. It's so good that you'll want to eat the whole batch yourself. The miso gives a memorable taste to these aubergines, which will almost be falling apart, for a moreish veggie side dish.

50ml olive oil

2 tbsp maple syrup

4 tsp tamari or soy sauce

3 tsp miso paste

2 large aubergines, diced into small chunks

Preheat the oven to 190°C.

Put the oil, maple syrup, tamari or soy sauce and miso in a bowl and stir to combine into a smooth sauce.

Put the aubergines in a large bowl, then pour over the sauce. Use your hands to rub it into the aubergines.

Transfer the aubergines to a baking dish to keep the juices in – it doesn't matter if they're on top of each other. Drizzle over any excess liquid from the bowl.

Bake in the pre-heated oven for 35 minutes. Serve hot.

Serves 4

STREET CORN

An easy side that's packed full of flavour. I sometimes make this for wrap fillers or even just to have on its own. Sweet, spicy, simple!

1 tbsp olive oil

½ a red onion, peeled and diced

200g frozen sweetcorn

1½ tsp ground cumin

1 tsp smoked paprika

2 handfuls of fresh flat-leaf parsley leaves, chopped

juice of 1 lime

sea salt and freshly ground black pepper

tortilla salad dressing (page 80)

Heat the oil in a frying pan over a high heat. Toss in the onion and cook, stirring constantly, for 2 minutes, until lightly browned but not burned.

Add the sweetcorn, cumin and paprika and cook for 4 to 5 minutes, until the corn is nicely browned.

Stir in the parsley and lime juice, then season to taste. Drizzle over the dressing and toss to coat. Serve hot.

POTATO SALAD

The perfect side for summer. The mix of sweet and white
potatoes gives this dish a different taste and with the homemade
mayo, it's a comforting addition to any plate.

2 potatoes (400g), peeled
  and diced

1 large sweet potato (200g),
  peeled and diced

**For the homemade
  vegan mayo:**

60g silken tofu

1 tbsp lemon juice

1 tsp Dijon mustard

pinch of sea salt

120ml olive oil or
  oil of choice

To garnish:

chopped fresh chives

Steam the potatoes until tender (see page 94). Set aside
until they are completely cool while you make the mayo.

To make the mayo, put the tofu, lemon juice, mustard and
salt in a blender or food processor and blend until smooth.
With the motor running, slowly add the oil little by little.
Once all the oil has been added, the mayo should have
thickened and emulsified.

Once the potatoes are completely cold, combine them with
the mayo. Chill in the fridge for 30 minutes before serving,
then garnish with chopped fresh chives.

SWEET AND SPICY EDAMAME

Remember the first time you ate edamame? Well, I do. I ate the whole thing (yep, the whole thing), wondering how anyone could like them. Then I realised that everyone at the table was putting the pods back in a bowl. Live and learn! My love for edamame has grown and grown since then. Plain or tarted up, they're the best starter or side to any meal.

1 tbsp sesame oil

4 garlic cloves, peeled and finely chopped

1 x 5cm piece of fresh ginger, peeled and finely chopped

1 tbsp chilli paste

200g cooked edamame in the pods

2 tbsp maple syrup

2 tbsp tamari or soy sauce

pinch of chilli flakes

pinch of sea salt

Heat the oil in a large frying pan over a high heat. Add the garlic, ginger and chilli paste and cook for 30 seconds. Toss in the edamame, then add the maple syrup and tamari or soy sauce. Stir to fully mix all the ingredients and cook for 1 minute.

Remove from the heat. Finish with a sprinkle of chilli flakes and salt.

VEGETABLE BAKE

This easy and reliable one-tray bake makes the best all-in-one side, perfect
for meal prep or a family. It takes only a few minutes to prep, then you can
forget about it while it bakes. I like to use the veggies listed below, but you
could use up any veg left in your fridge that might be on the way out.

8 baby potatoes, cut in
  half lengthways

8 cherry tomatoes,
  left whole

1 large courgette, sliced

100g button mushrooms,
  stems removed

2 tbsp olive oil

1½ tsp dried sage

1 tsp dried thyme

pinch of sea salt

Preheat the oven to 190°C.

Place all the ingredients in a baking dish, tossing to ensure
the vegetables are coated in the oil.

Roast in the oven for 35 minutes, until all the veg are tender.
Serve hot.

SWEET POTATO GRATIN

Make this with sweet potato, regular potato or any
veggies you like for a creamy, warming side.

1 tbsp oil

1 small onion, peeled
and grated

2 garlic cloves, peeled
and finely chopped

2 tbsp finely chopped
fresh flat-leaf parsley

130g cashews

250ml vegetable stock

3 tbsp nutritional yeast

good pinch of sea salt

½ tsp freshly ground
black pepper

3 large sweet potatoes
(600g), peeled and
sliced into thin rings
(I use a mandolin slicer)

Preheat the oven to 190°C.

Heat the oil in a frying pan over a high heat. Add the onion
and cook for 2 minutes, stirring constantly so that it doesn't
burn. Add the garlic and parsley and cook for 1 minute more,
then remove from the heat.

Put the cashews, stock and nutritional yeast in a blender
and blitz until smooth. Add the onion mix and the seasoning
and blend again for 30 seconds, until fully combined.

Put the sweet potato slices in a baking dish, making nice
layers, then pour over the cashew sauce. Tap the bottom
of the dish on the counter to make sure the sauce trickles
down through all the layers.

Bake in the preheated oven for 45 minutes. Serve hot.

BAKED BROCCOLI WITH CREAMY TAHINI DRESSING

I have a big bowl of this sometimes when I'm craving some greens. The broccoli is brought to life by the creamy dressing and crunchy seeds – it makes eating your greens far too easy.

1 head of broccoli,
  broken into florets

1 tbsp olive oil

pinch of sea salt

1 tsp freshly ground
  black pepper

80g pumpkin seeds

**For the creamy
  tahini dressing:**

juice of 1 lemon

2 tbsp water

2 tbsp tahini

1 tbsp apple cider vinegar

1 tbsp maple syrup

1 tsp Dijon mustard

Preheat the oven to 190°C.

In a bowl, toss the broccoli with the oil, salt and pepper. Tip out onto a baking tray and bake in the preheated oven for 20 minutes, until crisp on top and tender throughout (another option is to steam the broccoli). Add the pumpkin seeds to the tray for the last 10 minutes of the cooking time.

While the broccoli is cooking, make the tahini dressing. Put all the ingredients in a bowl and whisk together until smooth.

Remove the broccoli from the oven and tip into a serving bowl. Drizzle over the tahini dressing and serve hot.

Serves 4

STUFFED PORTOBELLOS

I can't wait for you to try these. They're perfect for snacks, sides or canapés. The mushroom caps are soft and juicy, and then there's the flavoursome filling – they cover all angles of taste bud satisfaction.

75g cashews

8 sun-dried tomatoes

juice of ½ a lemon

2 tbsp nutritional yeast

1 tbsp olive oil

½ a red onion, peeled and diced

2 handfuls of spinach leaves, finely chopped

4 large Portobello mushrooms, wiped clean

Preheat the oven to 190°C.

Put the cashews, sun-dried tomatoes, lemon juice and nutritional yeast in a blender and blitz into a chunky paste, then tip into a medium-sized bowl. Set aside.

Heat the oil in a frying pan over a high heat. Add the onion and cook for 2 minutes, until soft. Add the spinach and cook for 1 to 2 minutes, until wilted. Add to the bowl and stir to combine with the cashew mix.

Put the mushrooms face up on a baking tray and spoon 2 tablespoons of the mix into each one. Bake in the preheated oven for 30 minutes. Serve hot.

CREAMY MUSHROOM GRAVY

Spooned over pasta, veggie noodles, burgers or plain boiled rice, this creamy sauce is so delicious. It's perfect for adding a bit of life to dry meals.

2 tbsp oil, plus extra
  for cooking
1 tbsp balsamic vinegar
1 tsp miso paste (optional)
2 garlic cloves, peeled
  and crushed
250g button
  mushrooms, sliced
1 tsp dried thyme
½ tsp dried sage
250ml mushroom
  or vegetable stock
2 tbsp oat flour

Whisk together the oil, balsamic vinegar and miso paste (if using) in a small bowl.

Heat a splash of oil in a saucepan over a medium-high heat. Add the crushed garlic and cook for 30 seconds. Toss in the mushrooms and herbs and cook for 2 to 3 minutes, until the mushrooms have softened.

Pour in the stock and the miso mixture, then add the oat flour, stirring until there are no lumps. Simmer for 1 to 2 minutes to let the sauce thicken. Serve hot.

SNACKS

Hangry helpers

A lesson I've learned the hard way is not to go anywhere
for an uncertain amount of time without some snacks. I don't
know if anyone else suffers from hanger, the term coined
to describe someone who gets angry when they're hungry.
I carry multiple bags with me at any one time, so much so
that I'm often called the bag lady, but I guarantee that at
least one of those bags is just snacks. From planes to hikes,
be prepared! I've got you covered, whether you fancy
something sweet or savoury. My favourites are the quinoa
pizza muffins and the sausage rolls.

QUINOA PIZZA MUFFINS

These fluffy little savoury bites are perfect for a lunchbox
or when you're craving pizza on a Monday.

300g quinoa
4 tbsp chia seeds
12 tbsp plus 120ml water
60ml olive oil, plus extra
    for greasing
juice of ½ a lemon
5 tbsp nutritional yeast
½ tsp bicarbonate of soda
½ tsp sea salt
8 tbsp vegan basil pesto
    (page 86)
16 sun-dried tomatoes

Soak the quinoa in water overnight in the fridge. Grease a 12-cup muffin tray.

Preheat the oven to 180°C.

Put the chia seeds and 12 tablespoons of water in a small bowl and stir to combine. Set aside to soak for 15 minutes.

Drain the quinoa in a fine mesh sieve and rinse under cold running water, making sure you drain off all the excess water.

Put the quinoa and chia 'egg' in a food processor along with the 120ml of water, oil, lemon juice, nutritional yeast, bicarbonate of soda and salt. Blend until smooth, with no full bits of quinoa visible. It should look like a smooth batter with just a bit of texture.

Spoon 2½ tablespoons of the mix into each muffin cup. Add ½ tablespoon of pesto and top with a sun-dried tomato.

Bake in the preheated oven for 35 minutes. Allow to cool completely on a wire rack, still in the tray, then pop them out of the tray. Store any leftovers in an airtight container in the fridge for up to four days.

SAUSAGE ROLLS

Promise me you'll make these – they are so easy and unbelievably tasty.
This recipe also uses the one thing that I can never make myself: puff pastry.
Believe me, I've tried, but it's impossible! Luckily you can just pick up a roll
of vegan puff pastry in most supermarkets now to save yourself the trouble!

1 x 400g tin of chickpeas,
    drained and rinsed

50g pecans

50g whole almonds

1 tbsp olive oil, plus extra
    for drizzling

½ a large onion, peeled
    and grated

½ an apple, grated
    (skin on is fine)

1 large garlic clove, peeled
    and crushed

1 sprig of fresh rosemary,
    needles stripped
    and chopped

1 sprig of fresh thyme, leaves
    stripped and chopped

2 tbsp nutritional yeast
    (optional)

2 tbsp tomato purée

1 tbsp tamari or soy sauce

1 sheet of vegan puff pastry

handful of sesame seeds

Preheat the oven to 180°C. Line a baking tray with non-stick
baking paper.

Put the chickpeas in a food processor and blend until
smooth(ish). There will still be some chickpeas visible and
it will be a thick, lumpy paste. Spoon into a bowl.

Put the pecans and almonds in a high-speed blender (such
as a NutriBullet) and mill into a chunky flour. Set aside.

Heat the oil in a frying pan over a medium-high heat. Toss
in the onion, apple and garlic and cook for 2 minutes. Add
the herbs and cook for a further 1 to 2 minutes, until the
onion is golden and softened. Add to the chickpeas and
stir to combine.

Add the milled nuts to the chickpea mixture along with the
nutritional yeast (if using), tomato purée and the tamari or
soy sauce and stir again into a thick dough. It will be a little
wet, but it should still be easy to roll with your hands.

Unroll the pastry sheet onto a clean board and slice it lengthways
to make two long strips of pastry, stretching it just a little bit on
each side using your hands. Spoon the chickpea mixture into the
middle and mould it into a long sausage shape. Fold the pastry
over the filling, then press the edges of the pastry with your
fingers, sealing it tight. Slice into 12 mini sausage rolls.

Carefully lift the rolls onto the lined baking tray. Drizzle with a
little olive oil, then sprinkle over the sesame seeds. Bake in the
preheated oven for 25 minutes, until golden around the edges.

HAZELNUT AND RAISIN COOKIES

These remind me of the sort of cookie my grandparents used to get us for our weekend treat when we were growing up. They're thick, crunchy and chewy, with all the dunkability you could want.

2 tbsp milled flaxseeds

6 tbsp water

100g oats (porridge, rolled or jumbo oats will all work)

120g ground almonds

¾ tsp bicarbonate of soda

½ tsp baking powder

pinch of sea salt

60g coconut oil, melted

4 tbsp maple syrup

3 tbsp nut butter (I use peanut butter)

80g hazelnuts (toasted hazelnuts work best here)

80g raisins

Preheat the oven to 180°C. Line a baking tray with non-stick baking paper.

Put the milled flaxseeds and water in a small bowl and stir to combine. Set aside to soak for 15 minutes.

Put the oats in a food processor or high-speed blender (like a NutriBullet) and blitz into a flour. Tip into a large bowl and combine with the ground almonds, bicarbonate of soda, baking powder and salt.

In a separate bowl, mix together the coconut oil, maple syrup, nut butter and flax 'egg'. Add to the dry ingredients and stir to form a heavy, smooth dough. Lastly, stir in the hazelnuts and raisins.

Divide the dough into 12 portions and roll into even-sized balls. Place each ball on the lined tray and press down to create a cookie shape.

Bake in the preheated oven for 13 to 15 minutes, until golden all around the edges. Don't try to lift them off the tray straight away – leave them to cool for 10 minutes. During this time they will firm up and develop a lovely crunchy texture. After the 10 minutes are up, lift gently off the tray with a spatula. They're now ready to dunk in a mug of tea.

Store the cookies in an airtight container in the fridge for up to five days.

PROTEIN BARS

You didn't think I would skip the main attraction – protein bars – did you? They've been something of a favourite in my first two books. I find protein bars to be such a great snack on the go. They're perfect for carrying around in your bag, as they don't fall apart or smell. I usually whip up a batch of the no-bake bars, but you can also bake them as cookies instead.

200g cashew butter (tahini works too for a nut-free version)

160g maple syrup

90g vegan protein powder (use only 60g if making cookies)

100g vegan dark chocolate, chopped

If you want to make the no-bake bars, line a 1lb loaf tin with cling film or non-stick baking paper.

Put the cashew butter, maple syrup and protein powder in a bowl and stir to combine into a smooth dough. Spoon the dough into the lined tin, pressing it down evenly to flatten the top and form a bar shape.

Melt the chocolate in a heatproof bowl set over a saucepan of simmering water, making sure the water doesn't touch the bottom of the bowl. Drizzle over the melted chocolate, then put the tin in the fridge to set.

Cut as desired (I like to make 10 small bars). When cutting into bars, heat the knife with hot water first so that it slides through the hardened chocolate without cracking it. Store in an airtight container in the fridge for up to six days.

If you want to make cookies, preheat the oven to 180°C. Line a baking tray with non-stick baking paper.

Put the cashew butter, maple syrup and 60g of protein powder in a bowl and stir to combine into a smooth dough, then stir in the chopped chocolate.

Divide the dough into eight equal portions and roll into balls. Place on the lined baking tray and flatten them gently with your fingers. Bake in the preheated oven for 12 minutes. Allow to cool fully on a wire rack so that they set and firm up. When completely cool, store in an airtight container for up to three days.

PROTEIN MUFFIN

This has got to be the quickest dessert-like snack there is. It's so delicious that I make one on a Friday night after a long week, then sit down to catch up on my favourite shows. It's pure treat heaven made without any fuss.

5 tbsp nut milk

2 tbsp vegan chocolate protein powder

1 tbsp ground almonds

1 tbsp peanut butter, plus extra to serve

1 tbsp maple syrup

handful of vegan dark chocolate chips

To serve:

coconut yogurt

Put the nut milk, protein powder, ground almonds, peanut butter and maple syrup in a ramekin and stir to combine into a smooth batter, then stir in the chocolate chips.

Put the ramekin in the microwave and cook on high for 1 minute 40 seconds. It will rise up a little.

Allow to cool for a minute. Serve with a dollop of coconut yogurt on top and a little extra peanut butter for some more nutty goodness.

PEANUT CARAMEL BARS

A quick fix for Snickers fans, these mini bars are sweet,
peanutty goodness without much effort.

200g oats (porridge,
  rolled or jumbo oats
  will all work)

140g dates, pitted

100ml unsweetened
  almond milk

4 tbsp peanut butter

pinch of sea salt

For the topping:

300g vegan dark
  chocolate, chopped

1 to 2 tbsp coconut oil,
  melted (optional, but
  it helps to prevent the
  chocolate from setting
  too hard)

handful of roasted peanuts,
  roughly chopped

Line a 2lb loaf tin with cling film or non-stick baking paper.

Put the oats in a blender or food processor and blitz into
a flour. Add the dates and blend until the dates are broken
down into tiny pieces that are almost not visible. The mix
will have turned to a brownish colour. Add the almond milk,
peanut butter and salt and blend to combine into a thick
dough. Spoon the dough into the lined tin, pressing it down
evenly to flatten the top and form a bar shape.

To make the topping, melt the chocolate and coconut
oil together in a heatproof bowl set over a saucepan of
simmering water, making sure the water doesn't touch
the bottom of the bowl. Drizzle over the melted chocolate,
then scatter over the peanuts for a crunchy topping. Put
the tin in the freezer for 15 to 20 minutes or the fridge
for 45 minutes to set.

Cut as desired (I like to make eight bars). When cutting
into bars, heat the knife with hot water first so that it slides
through the hardened chocolate without cracking it. Store
in an airtight container in the fridge for up to six days.

BOOSTER BITES

If you hit the wall at 3pm, these little booster bites will get you back on track. The first time I trialled a batch I brought some in to my trainer and he was convinced that I had put caffeine powder in there!

300g oats (porridge, rolled or jumbo oats will all work)

300g dates, pitted

180ml unsweetened almond milk

3 tbsp cacao powder

1 tsp vanilla extract

pinch of sea salt

150g vegan dark chocolate

Line a 15cm square tin with non-stick baking paper.

Put the oats in a blender or food processor and blitz into a flour. Add the dates and blend until the dates are broken down into tiny pieces that are almost not visible. The mix will have turned to a brownish colour. Add the almond milk, cacao powder, vanilla and salt and blend to combine into a thick dough. Spoon the dough into the lined tin, pressing it down evenly to flatten the top.

To make the topping, melt the chocolate in a heatproof bowl set over a saucepan of simmering water, making sure the water doesn't touch the bottom of the bowl. Drizzle over the melted chocolate, then put the tin in the freezer for 15 to 20 minutes or the fridge for 45 minutes to allow the bars to set.

Cut as desired (I like to make 16 mini bites). When cutting into squares, heat the knife with hot water first so that it slides through the hardened chocolate without cracking it. Store in an airtight container in the fridge for up to six days.

ALMOND BUTTER BOMBS

These are a simple snack, perfect for meal prep. Make these
with whatever nut butter you have (I also like peanut butter)
or make them nut free by using tahini instead.

*185g oats (porridge, rolled or
jumbo oats will all work)*

5 tbsp nut milk

4 tbsp maple syrup

3 tbsp almond butter

pinch of sea salt

*50g vegan dark chocolate,
chopped*

*25g toasted almonds,
broken into chunks*

Put the oats in a blender or food processor and blitz into a
flour. Tip the flour out into a large bowl and add the nut milk,
maple syrup, almond butter and salt. Stir to combine into
a thick, smooth dough. Divide into 16 portions and roll into
balls. Set on a baking tray lined with non-stick baking paper.

Melt the chocolate in a heatproof bowl set over a saucepan
of simmering water, making sure the water doesn't touch the
bottom of the bowl. Pour 1 teaspoon of the melted chocolate
over each ball, letting it run down to coat the sides. Sprinkle
over the toasted almonds.

Put the tray in the freezer for 10 minutes or the fridge for
30 minutes to allow the balls to set. Store in an airtight
container in the fridge for up to five days.

Makes 18

CHICKPEA TRUFFLES

You heard it right, our favourite little beans are featuring in truffles now. Chickpeas have to be the most versatile ingredient, right? These truffles are soft, fudgy and fun – no one will believe you when you tell them they're made from chickpeas!

1 x 400g tin of chickpeas,
  drained and rinsed

100g peanut butter

4 tbsp cacao powder

3 tbsp maple syrup

1 tsp vanilla extract

pinch of sea salt

100g vegan dark
  chocolate, chopped

pinch of flaky sea salt
  (optional)

small handful of cacao
  nibs (optional)

Put the chickpeas, peanut butter, cacao powder, maple syrup, vanilla and salt in a food processor and blitz together until smooth. Divide into 18 portions and roll into balls. Set aside.

Line a baking tray with non-stick baking paper.

Melt the chocolate in a heatproof bowl set over a saucepan of simmering water, making sure the water doesn't touch the bottom of the bowl.

Using two forks, dip each truffle into the melted chocolate, then place on the lined baking tray. Scatter over a small pinch of flaky sea salt and/or cacao nibs (if using).

Place in the fridge for 1 hour to set. Store in an airtight container in the fridge for up to three days.

Makes 20 slices

CASHEW CHEESE

Are you missing a good Cheddar? If you love a cheese board, check this out. Loaded with fresh fruit, crackers and a vegan basil pesto, it's got it all going on. Agar agar is a vegetable setting agent and is available in health food stores or the Asian section of some supermarkets.

180g cashews
80ml unsweetened almond milk
juice of ½ a lemon
5 tbsp nutritional yeast
3 tbsp coconut oil, melted
1 tsp paprika
1 tsp garlic powder
1 tsp Dijon mustard
250ml water
4 tbsp agar agar

To serve:
fresh figs
fresh pears
crackers
vegan basil pesto (page 86)

Put the cashews, almond milk, lemon juice, nutritional yeast, melted coconut oil, paprika, garlic powder and Dijon mustard in a blender or food processor and blend until smooth and creamy.

Put the water and agar agar into a saucepan and bring to the boil, then lower the heat and simmer for 3 to 4 minutes, stirring occasionally, until the agar agar has dissolved. Pour the water into the blender or food processor and blitz again until smooth.

Pour the cashew cheese into a small baking dish or bowl lined with non-stick baking paper. Place in the fridge for 2 to 3 hours to set. Store in the fridge for up to five days.

Cut into slices and serve with fresh figs, pears, crackers and a small bowl of basil pesto.

TASTY TOFU BITES

I love having these prepped in advance as a savoury bite-sized snack. Or I sometimes cut them into strips and use them in spring rolls, add them to salads or serve on top of avocado toast.

2 tbsp tamari or soy sauce

2 tbsp maple syrup

1 tbsp hot sauce

1 tbsp sesame oil

400g firm tofu, diced into squares or sliced

Combine the tamari or soy sauce, maple syrup, hot sauce and sesame oil in a medium-sized bowl. Add the tofu pieces, gently stirring them around to coat in the marinade. Let the tofu sit in the marinade for as long as you can, but anything over 15 minutes is great.

Preheat the oven to 180°C. Line a baking tray with non-stick baking paper.

Transfer the tofu to the lined baking tray and bake in the preheated oven for 20 minutes. Serve hot or cold.

LENTIL BUNS

Snacking can be hard, especially when you're looking for a savoury option.
What's going to satisfy me and tide me over until my next meal? Hello, lentil buns.
They're filling, easy to pack in a lunchbox and – wait for it – don't smell, which is
really important in small offices and when having a cheeky snack on the bus!

1 tbsp olive oil, plus extra
for greasing.

½ an onion, peeled
and grated

2 garlic cloves, peeled
and crushed

1 small sweet potato (150g),
peeled and grated

2 x 400g tins of lentils,
drained and rinsed

100g walnuts (or you
could use porridge oats
as an alternative)

2 tbsp tomato purée

1 tbsp dried oregano

1 tbsp tamari or soy sauce

Preheat the oven to 190°C. Grease a 12-cup muffin tray.

Heat the oil in a frying pan over a high heat. Add the grated
onion and cook for 40 to 60 seconds, then add the garlic
and cook for 2 minutes. Add the sweet potato and cook for
4 minutes, stirring constantly. Remove the pan from the heat.

Put the sweet potato and onion mix in a blender or food
processor along with the lentils, walnuts, tomato purée, oregano
and the tamari or soy sauce and blend into a thick dough.

Spoon 3 to 4 tablespoons of the dough into each greased
muffin cup, filling it to the top. Bake in the preheated oven for
30 minutes. Allow to cool completely, then store in an airtight
container in the fridge for up to four days.

BREAD

Give us this day our daily . . .

Bread gets a really bad rap these days. Everyone's cutting out bread and blaming it for all their health problems, but maybe you just need to start making your own. I can also guarantee that the aroma of freshly baked bread will leave your house smelling delightful. I especially love the seeded oat loaf, or for a sweet slice, the banana bread is a winner.

CHOCOLATE BREAD

Okay, so maybe this should be in the dessert chapter, but a
bread's a bread and this one is awesome. I've even snuck a little
veg in there – it's the perfect treat to get them in!

2 tbsp milled flaxseeds

6 tbsp water

200g oats (porridge,
rolled or jumbo oats
will all work)

1 small to medium
courgette, grated

5 tbsp cacao powder

5 tbsp maple syrup

3 tbsp coconut oil, melted
(plus extra for greasing
if you're not lining the
tin with paper)

1 tsp baking powder

pinch of sea salt

80g vegan chocolate chips

Put the milled flaxseeds and water in a small bowl and stir
to combine. Set aside to soak for 15 minutes.

Preheat the oven to 180°C. Grease a 1lb loaf tin or line
with non-stick baking paper.

Start by milling your oats in a food processor or high-speed
blender (I use a NutriBullet) to a flour consistency. Tip into
a large bowl and add the flax 'egg' along with the grated
courgette, cacao powder, maple syrup, melted coconut oil,
baking powder and salt. Stir to combine, then stir in the
chocolate chips.

Scrape into the prepared tin and gently even out the top.
Bake in the preheated oven for 50 minutes.

Remove from the tin and allow to cool fully on a wire rack
for at least 1 hour before slicing and diving in. Store the
completely cooled bread in an airtight container for up to
four days.

BANANA BREAD

You can never have enough banana bread recipes – or at least that's what I like to tell myself! This recipe is so easy and you won't believe how good it tastes. I've made this version nut-free, but you can swap the tahini for your favourite nut butter or the chocolate chips for some toasted nuts.

200g oats (porridge, rolled or jumbo oats will all work)

1½ tsp baking powder

3 large ripe or overripe bananas, mashed

4 tbsp tahini

3½ tbsp maple syrup

3 tbsp coconut oil, melted

50ml unsweetened non-dairy milk

handful of vegan chocolate chips

To decorate:

1 ripe banana, sliced lengthways

Preheat the oven to 180°C. Grease a 1lb loaf tin or line with non-stick baking paper.

Start by milling your oats in a food processor or high-speed blender (I use a NutriBullet) to a flour consistency. Tip into a medium-sized bowl along with the baking powder.

In a separate bowl, mash the bananas really well until no large bits are visible. Stir in the tahini, maple syrup and melted coconut oil until fully combined. Pour the wet ingredients into the oat flour and stir until fully combined. The batter will be thick and a little dry at this point. Add the almond milk and stir until a sticky batter is formed.

Scrape into the prepared tin and gently even out the top. Place the banana slices on top, then scatter the chocolate chips around the banana slices. Bake in the preheated oven for 50 minutes, until golden brown and a skewer inserted into the centre comes out clean.

Remove from the tin and allow to cool on a wire rack for 30 to 45 minutes before slicing and digging in. Store the completely cooled bread in an airtight container for up to four days.

QUINOA BREAD

This is my go-to meal prep bread. The quinoa gives it a great texture.
Loaded up with sweet or savoury toppings, it's a real favourite of mine.

300g quinoa (try to
find a pack of
pre-washed quinoa)

100g oats (porridge,
rolled or jumbo oats
will all work)

50g sunflower seeds or
any other seeds you like
(or omit altogether)

250ml unsweetened
almond milk

1½ tsp dried thyme

2 tbsp maple syrup

2 tbsp olive oil

1 tbsp dried rosemary

1 tbsp apple cider vinegar

¾ tsp bicarbonate of soda

pinch of sea salt

Preheat the oven to 180°C. Grease a 1lb loaf tin or line with
non-stick baking paper.

Start by milling your quinoa and oats in a food processor or
high-speed blender (I use a NutriBullet) to a super-fine flour
consistency. Tip into a large bowl along with all the other
ingredients. Use a wooden spoon to combine into a thick,
sticky batter.

Scrape into the prepared tin and gently even out the top.
Bake in the preheated oven for 1 hour. Loosely cover the
top with tin foil after the first 35 minutes so that the bread
doesn't get too browned.

Remove from the tin and allow to cool on a wire rack for
30 minutes before slicing and digging in. Store the completely
cooled bread in an airtight container for up to four days. This
also freezes well – I recommend slicing it first and freezing in
sections, toasting individual slices as you need them.

SEEDED OAT LOAF

When I make a loaf of this bread, it's gone within a day in my house. It's
so irresistibly good that I can't help myself from having a slice every time
I pass the kitchen. I love it with a little coconut butter, pesto, mashed
avocado or dunked into soup. I sometimes make it with only pumpkin seeds
or only sunflower seeds and it gives this bread a complete makeover, as
they both taste totally different. I'm still not sure which one I like best!

*250g oats (porridge,
rolled or jumbo oats
will all work)*

*150g pumpkin or sunflower
seeds (or a mix of both),
plus extra for topping*

1 tbsp dried rosemary

½ tsp bicarbonate of soda

½ tsp baking powder

*250ml unsweetened
almond milk*

1 tbsp apple cider vinegar

2 tbsp coconut oil

2 tbsp maple syrup

Preheat the oven to 190°C. Line a ½lb loaf tin with non-stick
baking paper. I use a small tin to make a nice high loaf. You
can use a 1lb tin if that's all you have, but the loaf will be
short and wide instead.

Start by milling your oats and seeds in a food processor
or high-speed blender (I use a NutriBullet) to a flour
consistency. Tip into a large bowl along with the rosemary,
bicarbonate of soda and baking powder and stir to combine.

In a separate small bowl, combine the almond milk and
apple cider vinegar, then pour into the flour, mixing until
fully combined.

Melt the coconut oil and maple syrup together, then add
to the flour mixture, stirring to mix all the ingredients until
you have a smooth, thick batter.

Scrape into the prepared tin and gently even out the top,
then sprinkle over some extra pumpkin or sunflower seeds.
Bake in the preheated oven for 45 minutes.

Remove from the tin and allow to cool completely on a
wire rack before slicing. The bread sets when cooled and
tastes much nicer, so don't worry, you're not missing out
on anything by waiting. Store the completely cooled bread
in an airtight container for up to five days. It's also freezer
friendly, but I suggest cutting it into slices before freezing.

Makes 4

EVERYDAY OAT AND CHIA SCONES

These easy everyday scones are perfect for breakfast on the go or
an afternoon snack. I love them with chia jam (either the blackberry
one on page 59 or the raspberry one on page 235) and almond butter
or go savoury with mashed avocado and pesto (page 86).

*250g oats (porridge,
    rolled or jumbo oats
    will all work)*

160ml oat milk

1½ tbsp chia seeds

1 tbsp maple syrup

1 tsp baking powder

Preheat the oven to 180°C. Line a baking tray with non-stick
baking paper.

Start by milling your oats in a food processor or high-speed
blender (I use a NutriBullet) to a flour consistency. Tip into
a large bowl with all the other ingredients and stir to combine
into a wet dough.

Using a spoon, scoop the dough into four sections on the
baking tray to form scones, pressing each one down a little.
Bake in the preheated oven for 25 minutes.

Allow to cool a little on a wire rack before cutting in half
and serving however you like them best.

DESSERT

Treat yoself!

About seven years ago my sister and I had just enjoyed
a great day in Dublin. We'd had a family lunch and were
on the way home to Tipperary when we got in a car crash
(which wasn't our fault, I hasten to add). It was a bad
accident, life-flashing-before-your-eyes kind of stuff.
I remember thinking of my friends and all the things I
wanted to do that summer. My sister? She said that all
she thought was, 'I'm so glad I got dessert at lunch.' Now
I think about that every time I debate having dessert!

It's so hard to say what my favourite desserts are, but
if I had to, I'd pick the carrot cake, trillionaire's slice
and all the cups.

SWEET POTATO BROWNIES

Fudgy with a little bit of veg, it could only be an NBF brownie.
This easy all-in-one mix is the perfect recipe to start your baking
journey, as these brownies are foolproof and delicious.

*1 large sweet potato (300g),
   peeled and diced*

6 tbsp nut butter

5 tbsp maple syrup

4 tbsp cacao powder

1 tsp vanilla extract

pinch of sea salt

100g vegan chocolate chips

**For the chocolate
   topping:**

*1 x 400ml tin of full-fat
   coconut milk*

*100g vegan dark
   chocolate, chopped*

Put the tin of coconut milk in the fridge for 30 minutes to
let the cream rise to the top and harden. Without shaking
the tin, open it up and scoop the coconut cream off the top –
you need 2 tablespoons for this recipe.

Preheat the oven to 180°C. Line a 15cm square brownie tin
with non-stick baking paper.

You can steam the sweet potato in the microwave (see page
94) or over the hob until tender. Pop into a blender and
purée until smooth, then add the rest of the ingredients
except the chocolate chips and blend again until combined
into a smooth batter. Stir in the chocolate chips.

Spoon the batter into the lined tin. Bake in the preheated
oven for 22 minutes. Allow to cool on a wire rack.

Meanwhile, to make the chocolate topping, melt the chocolate
in a heatproof bowl set over a saucepan of simmering water,
making sure the bottom of the bowl doesn't touch the water.
Once the chocolate has melted, stir in the coconut cream. The
chocolate will thicken up, almost like a frosting. Spoon over the
cooled brownies and spread evenly. Allow to set before cutting
into nine squares.

BLONDIES, TWO WAYS

I love blondies, maybe even a little more than brownies. This is a fudgy caramel square with two ways to tickle your fancy: summer berries or chocolate chips.

200g ground almonds

4 tbsp almond butter

3 tbsp coconut sugar

3 tbsp maple syrup

3 tbsp unsweetened almond milk

2 tbsp coconut oil, melted

1 tsp baking powder

70g vegan chocolate chips or 4 tbsp chia jam (blackberry on page 59 or raspberry on page 235)

Preheat the oven to 180°C. Line a 2lb loaf tin with non-stick baking paper.

Put all the ingredients except the chocolate chips or jam in a large bowl and stir to combine into a thick, smooth batter.

If you're using the chocolate chips, stir them in, then spoon the batter into the lined tin and even out the top.

If you're going for the summer berry blondies, spoon the batter into the lined tin, then dot over tablespoons of the chia jam. Using a knife or the end of a spoon, swirl the top just a little to mix in the jam.

Bake in the preheated oven for 30 minutes. Allow to cool before cutting into eight pieces. Keep in an airtight container for up to five days.

NO-BAKE HAZELNUT CHEESECAKE

Two things everyone loves – hazelnuts and cheesecake – combined to create
a crowd-pleasing dessert. You can make this well in advance and store it in the
freezer for a fantastic make-ahead dessert for a dinner party. A little goes a long
way and the cheesecake is tall, which is why you can cut it into so many slices.

400g raw unsalted cashews
5 tbsp cacao powder
150ml maple syrup
4 tbsp coconut oil

For the base:
150g Medjool dates, pitted
100g almonds
100g hazelnuts
2 tbsp cacao powder
pinch of sea salt

For the ganache:
1 x 400ml tin of full-fat
  coconut milk
200g vegan dark chocolate,
  roughly chopped
3 tbsp coconut oil

To decorate:
100g roasted hazelnuts,
  roughly chopped
pinch of flaky sea salt

Put the cashews in a small bowl and cover them with water.
Soak for at least 5 hours or overnight. Drain well.

Put the tin of coconut milk in the fridge for 30 minutes to
let the cream rise to the top and harden. Without shaking
the tin, open it up and scoop the coconut cream off the top
– you need 4 tablespoons for this recipe.

Grease and line a 20cm round springform tin with non-stick
baking paper.

Put all the base ingredients in a blender or food processor
and blitz to combine. Tip into the prepared springform tin
and use your hands to press down evenly over the bottom
of the tin.

Put the soaked cashews, cacao powder, maple syrup and
coconut oil in a blender or food processor and blitz until
smooth. Pour over the base and shake the tin a little to
even out the top. Place in the fridge for at least 2 hours
or overnight to set.

When you're nearly ready to serve, make the ganache.

Melt the chocolate and coconut oil in a heatproof bowl set
over a saucepan of simmering water, making sure the bottom
of the bowl doesn't touch the water. Once the chocolate
has melted, let it cool a little before stirring in the coconut
cream. The sauce will become thick and creamy. If the

coconut splits because the chocolate was too hot, don't worry – just blitz the mix in a high-speed blender, such as a NutriBullet, to bring it back together.

Remove the cake from the springform tin and immediately spread the ganache across the top. Sprinkle with the chopped roasted hazelnuts and flaky sea salt and cut into slices.

Store the cheesecake in the fridge for up to six days or in the freezer for up to two weeks.

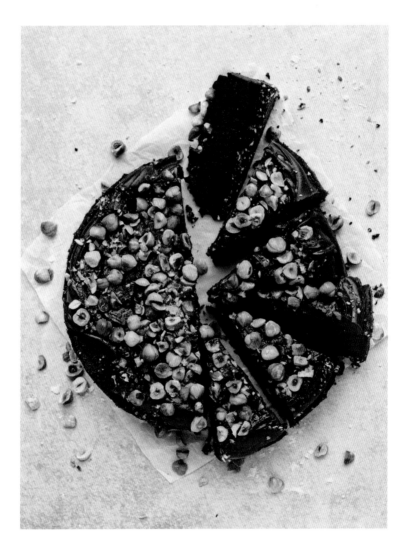

CLASSIC BLUEBERRY
BAKED CHEESECAKE

My dad used to make the most delicious cheesecake, full of condensed milk and cream cheese – not vegan at all! So I decided to have a bake-off by making an even more indulgent and tasty doppelgänger to bring down to my family. It was challenging to recreate a dessert that's so familiar to all of us, but here it is, zesty, nostalgic and made from tofu!

400g raw unsalted cashews

400g firm tofu

125ml maple syrup

125ml nut milk

zest and juice of 3 lemons

1 tbsp nutritional yeast (optional)

For the base:

1 tbsp milled flaxseeds

3 tbsp water

100g oats (porridge, rolled or jumbo oats will all work)

100g ground almonds

4 tbsp coconut oil

2 tbsp maple syrup

For the blueberry chia jam:

250g fresh or frozen blueberries

2 to 3 tbsp maple syrup

2 tbsp chia seeds

Put the cashews in a small bowl and cover them with water. Soak for at least 5 hours or overnight. Drain well.

To make the chia jam, put the blueberries in a small saucepan over a medium heat and mash with a fork. Allow to simmer for 3 to 4 minutes, stirring occasionally. Stir in the maple syrup and chia seeds, then remove the pan from the heat and set aside to allow the jam to thicken.

Preheat the oven to 180°C. Grease and line a 20cm round springform tin with non-stick baking paper.

To make the base, put the milled flaxseeds and water in a medium-sized bowl and stir to combine. Set aside to soak for 15 minutes.

To make the base, put the flax 'egg', oats, ground almonds, coconut oil and maple syrup in a bowl and stir to combine. Tip into the prepared springform tin and use your hands to press down evenly over the bottom of the tin.

Put all the cheesecake ingredients, including the soaked cashews, in a blender or food processor and blitz until silky smooth. Spoon this thick sauce over the base and smooth out the top as best you can. Spoon over the blueberry chia jam and swirl it into the top of the cheesecake.

Bake in the preheated oven for 40 minutes, until almost completely firm. Allow to cool on a wire rack before releasing the cheesecake from the springform tin and cutting into slices.

SHORTBREAD BISCUITS

Go forth and make these! They have honestly been the number-one hit among my friends. Plus the fact that they are super-easy to make means you really have no excuse. I just suggest you make a double batch, as they go too fast.

125g porridge oats
60g ground almonds
3 tbsp maple syrup
3 tbsp coconut oil, melted
pinch of sea salt
8 squares of vegan
  chocolate (optional)

To serve:

melted vegan dark
  chocolate
orange zest
lime zest
cacao nibs
pinch of flaky sea salt

Preheat the oven to 180°C. Line a baking tray with non-stick baking paper.

Put the oats in a food processor and blitz into a fine flour. Tip into a bowl and add the ground almonds, maple syrup, melted coconut oil and salt. Mix to combine into a dough.

Divide into eight portions and roll each one into a ball. Place on the lined tray, then press down into a cookie shape. Press a square of chocolate on top of each one (if using).

Bake in the preheated oven for 17 to 18 minutes, until golden around the edges. Allow to cool on the tray for 10 minutes before carefully lifting them off.

For an extra treat, dip the biscuits in a little pot of melted chocolate, then scatter with orange zest, lime zest, cacao nibs and a pinch of flaky sea salt.

Makes 8

CHOCOLATE PROTEIN DONUTS

Pure delight in every bite. These are fluffy on the inside with a nice crisp shell. The topping is the key player here that takes these to the next level.

150g apple sauce

125g ground almonds

40g vegan chocolate protein powder

4 tbsp melted coconut oil, plus extra for greasing

2 tbsp coconut sugar or stevia

2 tbsp cacao powder

1 tbsp apple cider vinegar

½ tsp baking powder

¼ tsp bicarbonate of soda

For the topping:

2 tbsp cashew butter

1 tbsp coconut sugar

1 tbsp melted coconut oil

Preheat the oven to 180°C. Lightly grease a donut mould.

Combine all the donut ingredients in a bowl, mixing well to create a smooth batter, then spoon into the donut tin. Smooth over the top.

Bake in the preheated oven for 15 to 20 minutes, until firm around edges. Leave them in the tin to cool fully before lifting them out. Trust me, they're nicer cold – the edges are crisp and the inside is fluffy and moist.

To make the topping, combine all the ingredients in a small bowl. Place in the fridge to harden up a bit, then use a knife to spread on top of each cooled donut. If I was preparing these for friends or a party, I would wait until serving to load on the topping.

Store the donuts in an airtight container in the fridge for up to three days.

CARROT CAKE

What's the one dessert you can't resist? For me, it's carrot cake. I used to be a banoffee girl (I've got an awesome vegan version in my first book), but these days, there's something about the nutty, sweet sponge and frosting that gets me every time. I can't wait to see your recreations of this. As my boyfriend said, this just had to be in the book.

100g walnut halves

200g oats (porridge, rolled or jumbo oats will all work)

100g ground almonds

80g coconut sugar

1 tsp ground cinnamon

1 tsp ground nutmeg

1 tsp baking powder

¾ tsp bicarbonate of soda

150ml olive oil or oil of choice

1 tbsp apple cider vinegar

1 tsp vanilla extract

200g grated carrots

60g raisins

cashew mascarpone (page 59), to ice

To decorate:

toasted walnut halves

zest of ½ an orange

Preheat the oven to 180°C. Line a 15cm round tin with non-stick baking paper.

Start by putting the walnuts on a small baking tray and toasting in the preheated oven for 12 to 15 minutes, until they've turned golden around the edges. Tip out onto a plate and set aside to cool.

Mill your oats in a food processor or high-speed blender (I use a NutriBullet) to a flour consistency. Tip into a large bowl with the ground almonds, coconut sugar, spices, baking powder and bicarbonate of soda and mix well.

Combine the oil, vinegar and vanilla in a jug, then pour into the dry ingredients. Stir to combine into a smooth, thick batter. Fold in the toasted walnuts, grated carrot and raisins.

Spoon the batter into the lined tin, smoothing out the top with the back of a spoon. Bake in the oven for 30 minutes.

Leave to cool fully before lifting the cake out of the tin. It tastes much better once cooled, so don't worry, you're not missing out by waiting. Cover the top with a layer of cashew mascarpone, then decorate with walnut halves and orange zest. Cut into slices to serve.

BLUEBERRY CRUMBLE

You can't beat a good crumble for a fuss-free dessert that's perfect
for any dinner party. I made this for my sister's engagement dinner
along with a very, very time-consuming lemon soufflé that no one
mentioned afterwards – they only raved about this crumble. Typical!

600g fresh or frozen
  blueberries

juice of 1 orange

3 tbsp maple syrup

**For the crumble
  topping:**

200g ground almonds

100g oats (porridge,
  rolled or jumbo oats
  will all work)

60g seeds

50g chopped nuts

4 tbsp coconut sugar

2 tbsp coconut oil, melted

Preheat the oven to 180°C.

Put the berries, orange juice and maple syrup in a baking
dish and stir to combine.

In a separate bowl, mix together all the ingredients for
the crumble topping. Use your hands to sprinkle it over
the berries, making sure you cover them fully.

Bake in the preheated oven for 45 minutes. Serve warm.

RASPBERRY AND PISTACHIO POPSICLES

The perfect summer treat, refreshing and waiting
in the freezer whenever you're ready!

*25g finely chopped
roasted pistachios
(or nut of choice)*

*200g fresh raspberries
(or berries of choice)*

300g coconut yogurt

juice of 2 limes

2 tbsp maple syrup

Start by dividing the pistachios evenly between six
popsicle moulds.

Put the raspberries in a small bowl and mash with the
back of a fork until smooth.

In a separate bowl, combine the coconut yogurt, lime juice
and maple syrup. Add 2 tablespoons of the yogurt to each
mould, tapping the mould so that it sits in the bottom and
fully coats the pistachios. Follow by adding 1 tablespoon of
the mashed raspberries. Repeat with another 2 tablespoons
of yogurt, then finish with 1 tablespoon of mashed raspberries.

Place in the freezer for at least 3 hours or overnight,
until frozen.

TRILLIONAIRE'S SLICE

My first book has a billionaire's shortbread, so it's only right that this book brings this treat to its ultimate level. With a more satisfying divide between the layers and a creamy caramel, these trump the lot.

For the base:

200g Medjool dates, pitted

125g oats (porridge, rolled or jumbo oats will all work)

100g nuts (I like almonds or you can make it nut-free by using mixed seeds)

pinch of sea salt

For the caramel:

200g raw unsalted cashews (or use 4 tbsp tahini if making a nut-free version)

200g Medjool dates, pitted

1 tsp sea salt

1 tsp vanilla extract

For the chocolate topping:

1 x 400ml tin of full-fat coconut milk

200g vegan dark chocolate, chopped

2 tbsp coconut oil

Place the cashews for the caramel in a bowl and cover to the top with water. Allow to soak for at least 3 hours, then drain well.

Put the tin of coconut milk for the chocolate topping in the fridge for 30 minutes to let the cream rise to the top and harden. Without shaking the tin, open it up and scoop the coconut cream off the top – you need 4 tablespoons for this recipe. The cream will be hard, so put it in a bowl and whisk until smooth, with no lumps.

Grease and line a 20cm square baking tin with non-stick baking paper.

Put all the base ingredients in a food processor and blitz to combine into a sticky dough. Depending on your food processor this could take up to 4 or 5 minutes on high speed to reach this consistency. Tip into the lined tin and press down to create an even surface.

Put all the caramel ingredients in the blender, including the soaked and drained cashews or tahini, and blitz until silky smooth. Spoon on top of the base and smooth out to create an even layer.

To make the topping, melt the chocolate and coconut oil in a heatproof bowl set over a saucepan of simmering water, making sure the bottom of the bowl doesn't touch the water. Once the chocolate has melted, let it cool a little before stirring in the coconut cream. The sauce will become thick and creamy. If the coconut splits because the chocolate was too hot, don't worry – just blitz the mix in a high-speed blender, such as a NutriBullet, to bring it back together.

Pour the chocolate sauce over the caramel to create a smooth surface. Put the tin in the fridge for at least 2 hours, until set.

Remove the tin from the fridge 5 minutes before slicing so that the chocolate will soften a little and be easier to cut into 16 squares. Store in the fridge in an airtight container for up to six days.

COOKIE DOUGH SLICE

I had to! I cover the dough with a hard chocolate layer, finished off by
a chewy, crunchy cookie on top. It's the ultimate cookie lover's dessert.

250g ground almonds

8 tbsp maple syrup

4 tbsp almond butter,
    peanut butter or tahini

3 tbsp coconut flour

2 tbsp coconut oil, melted

pinch of sea salt

100g vegan chocolate chips

**For the chocolate
    topping:**

200g vegan dark
    chocolate, chopped

2 tbsp coconut oil

Preheat the oven to 180°C. Line a baking tray and a 16cm
square brownie tin with non-stick baking paper.

Put the ground almonds, maple syrup, nut butter or tahini,
coconut flour, melted coconut oil and salt in a bowl and stir
to combine, then stir in the chocolate chips.

Divide the mixture into two portions, making one portion a little
bigger than the other (two-thirds of the mix will be flattened and
the other one-third will be made into cookies). Take the largest
portion and press it down evenly over the base of the brownie tin
using a spatula. Leave a small gap along the edges.

To make the chocolate topping, melt the chocolate and coconut
oil together in a heatproof bowl set over a saucepan of simmering
water, making sure the bottom of the bowl doesn't touch the
water. Pour this over the cookie dough base in the brownie tin,
letting it spill down into the gap at the sides.

Divide the remaining dough into nine even portions and roll
them into golf ball-sized balls. Place on the lined baking tray and
press down into cookies. Bake in the preheated oven for 10 to 12
minutes, until golden brown around the edges.

Allow the cookies to cool on the tray for 5 to 10 minutes to firm
up before using a spatula to gently lift them from the tray. Place
the cookies on the top of the melted chocolate in the brownie
tin, spaced evenly apart. At this stage the chocolate will have
cooled a little but should not be fully set, so the heat from the
cookies will melt a nest into the chocolate layer.

Place the brownie tin in the fridge for 1 hour to set before slicing
into nine squares. Store in the fridge for up to one week.

THE BEST VEGAN CHOCOLATE CUPCAKES

Really good cupcakes have been the hardest vegan dessert to recreate using my beloved cupboard essentials, but these have yet to be topped. They're light, fluffy and a little bit indulgent, especially with the avocado frosting.

200g apple sauce

160g smooth peanut butter or almond butter

100g ground almonds

4 tbsp coconut oil, melted

3 tbsp cacao powder

2 tbsp maple syrup

¾ tsp baking powder

40g vegan chocolate, cut into pieces to make chocolate chunks

For the frosting (optional):

2 ripe avocados, peeled, stoned and halved

4 tbsp cacao powder

4 tbsp maple syrup

Preheat the oven to 180°C. Line six cups of a muffin tray with paper cases.

Put all the cupcake ingredients except the chocolate in a large bowl and stir to combine into a smooth batter, then fold in the chocolate chips.

Spoon 2 tablespoons of the batter into each paper case, then bake in the preheated oven for 25 minutes. Allow to cool completely before icing.

If you're making the frosting, simply blend everything together until smooth, then slather onto the cooled muffins. Adding the frosting lowers the life span of the cupcakes, though, as avocados are so temperamental. If you're planning on keeping these for a few days, you might want to opt for the brownie ganache on page 208 instead.

Store unfrosted cupcakes in an airtight container for up to five days.

Makes 8

THE ULTIMATE
CHOCOLATE COOKIE

The soft cookie with crunchy toasted nuts is so indulgent. I love making these on a Saturday and hoard them all for myself. Sorry, but they're too good to share.

1 tbsp milled flaxseeds

3 tbsp water

6 tbsp smooth cashew butter

5 tbsp maple syrup

4 tbsp cacao powder

3 tbsp coconut oil, at room temperature

½ tsp baking powder

60g whole nuts, toasted (walnuts, pecans, hazelnuts or macadamia nuts work best)

50g vegan dark chocolate, broken into chunks

Preheat the oven to 180°C. Line a baking tray with non-stick baking paper.

Put the milled flaxseeds and water in a medium-sized bowl and stir to combine. Set aside to soak for 15 minutes.

Once the flax 'egg' is ready, add the cashew butter, maple syrup, cacao powder, coconut oil and baking powder to the same bowl and mix well using a spoon or fork, then stir in the toasted nuts and chocolate chunks.

Using two dessertspoons, take a heaped spoonful of dough, then scrape it off onto the lined tray using the other spoon. You don't need to shape them or flatten them out. You should have enough dough to make eight cookies.

Bake in the preheated oven for 10 minutes. Leave to cool and firm up on the tray for 10 minutes before digging in.

PROTEIN ALMOND CRUNCH CUPS

I am all for anything that comes in a cup. These have a delicious chocolate layer followed by a protein-packed, truffle-like filling, all in one crisp bite. Is your mouth watering yet? The filling also makes awesome energy balls.

80g vegan protein powder (vanilla works best here)

8 level tbsp almond butter

6 tbsp maple syrup

2 tbsp roughly chopped toasted almonds

For the chocolate cups:

300g vegan dark chocolate, chopped

2 tbsp coconut oil

These work best if you use a silicone cupcake tin, but if you don't have one, set out 10 paper cupcake cases in a baking tin or something similar that will fit in your freezer so that they keep their shape and don't spill.

Melt the chocolate in a heatproof bowl set over a saucepan of simmering water, making sure the bottom of the bowl doesn't touch the water. Stir the coconut oil into the melted chocolate until well combined. Spoon 1 tablespoon of melted chocolate into the bottom of each cupcake mould or paper case, then set in the freezer to harden. You'll be using the rest of the melted chocolate later, so keep it warm.

Meanwhile, put the protein powder, almond butter and maple syrup in a bowl and stir to combine into a dough. It should be wet enough to stick together but not dry enough that it falls apart if you try to roll it into a ball. If it is too dry, which can happen depending on what type of protein powder you use – for example, whey can be more powdery – just add a little more nut butter or maple syrup. Finally, stir in the almonds. Divide the mix into roughly 10 even portions and roll into balls, then press lightly into small, thick cookies. They'll be a tad sticky, but don't worry.

Place a cookie on top of each hardened chocolate base, then spoon over the rest of the melted chocolate, dividing it evenly between the 10 cups. Pop back in the freezer for 15 minutes to set.

Once set, store the cups in the fridge in an airtight container for up to two weeks.

KINDA NUTTY CUPS

I think you already know how good these are going to taste. The epic crunch and sweet nutty aftertaste are a killer combo. I make these into cups (see the photo on page 231), but you can also make these into bars by pressing into a large loaf tin – however, I have to warn you that they can be tricky to cut, so the cups work far easier.

300g mixed nuts (if using hazelnuts or peanuts, go for the skinless kind or just remove the skins yourself after toasting)

1 tsp sea salt

120ml maple syrup

60g vegan chocolate (optional)

Preheat the oven to 190°C.

Spread the nuts on a baking tray and toast in the preheated oven for 15 minutes. (If you are using hazelnuts or peanuts with the skin on, put them on a separate tray to make it easier to skin them.) Remove any skins if necessary. Tip the nuts into a bowl with the salt and stir to coat.

Put the maple syrup in a saucepan over a high heat. Bring to the boil, then continue to let it boil for about 4 minutes, stirring every 40 seconds. Try not to let the maple catch and burn at the bottom. The goal is to get the maple syrup reduced to a thick, heavy syrup – when you stir it, it will be almost stringy. When it's ready, pour the maple syrup over the nuts and quickly stir them together.

Spoon the glazed nuts into eight holes of a muffin tray (which doesn't need to be lined or greased), pressing down with the back of the spoon to pack them tightly.

Place in the freezer for 15 minutes or in the fridge for 45 minutes to set. Once cold, you can loosen the cups using a knife and they should pop out. These will be seriously crunchy, so watch your gnashers! Store in an airtight container in the fridge for up to 10 days.

Makes 12

COOKIE DOUGH CUPS

I remember having cookie dough for the first time in America and thinking that I was never allowed to eat the dough at home! I love to use this cookie dough in chocolate cups, as here, but also in banana ice cream or simply rolled up into balls for a delicious bite.

For the chocolate casing:

375g vegan dark chocolate, finely chopped

3 tbsp coconut oil

For the filling:

½ x 400g tin of chickpeas, drained and rinsed

35g oats (porridge, rolled or jumbo oats will all work)

75ml maple syrup

2 tbsp peanut butter

pinch of sea salt

25g vegan dark chocolate, finely chopped

Line a 12-hole muffin tray with paper cases.

To make the chocolate casing, melt the chocolate and coconut oil together in a heatproof bowl set over a saucepan of simmering water, making sure the water doesn't touch the bottom of the bowl.

Add 2 teaspoons of the melted chocolate to each paper case. Using a pastry brush, brush the chocolate up the sides of the cases to evenly coat. Place in the freezer for 10 minutes to set. Repeat this process twice more. You'll still have melted chocolate left over, which you'll be using as the final layer.

While the chocolate casings are setting, put all the filling ingredients except the chocolate in a food processor and blitz to combine into a smooth dough. Stir in the finely chopped chocolate.

Divide the cookie dough evenly between the cups, pressing down to smooth out the tops. Top with the remaining melted chocolate and place back in the freezer for 30 minutes, until hardened.

Once set, remove the cups from the freezer and store in the fridge for up to four days.

BAKEWELL

This one is for my friend Seanie, who I shoot YouTube recipes with. Every day his Bakewell request gets shoved to one side, so Seanie, this is for you!

For the raspberry chia jam:

250g fresh or frozen raspberries

2 to 3 tbsp maple syrup

2 tbsp chia seeds

For the base:

1 tbsp milled flaxseeds

3 tbsp water

100g oats (porridge, rolled or jumbo oats will all work)

150g ground almonds

4 tbsp coconut oil

2 tbsp maple syrup

For the cake:

150g ground almonds

125g oats (porridge, rolled or jumbo oats will all work)

150ml unsweetened almond milk

4 tbsp coconut oil

2 tbsp maple syrup

1 tsp baking powder

1 tsp almond extract

To decorate:

25g flaked almonds

First make the chia jam. Put the raspberries in a small saucepan over a medium heat and mash with a fork. Allow to simmer for 3 to 4 minutes, stirring occasionally. Stir in the maple syrup and the chia seeds, then remove the pan from the heat and let it sit for 20 minutes to thicken.

Put the flaxseeds and water for the base in a small bowl and set aside for 15 minutes to plump up.

Preheat the oven to 180°C. Grease and line a 20cm square baking tin with non-stick baking paper.

To make the base, put the oats in a blender or food processor and blend into a flour. Add the ground almonds, coconut oil, maple syrup and the flax 'egg' and blend again into a dough. Tip the dough out into the lined tin and press it down in an even layer over the base. Bake in the preheated oven for 8 to 10 minutes, until golden brown.

Remove the tin from the oven and spoon the chia jam over the base.

Put all the cake ingredients in the blender or food processor and blitz into a smooth batter. Working quickly, as this will thicken if it's left to sit, dot the batter over the chia jam. Gently spread it out in an even layer, then sprinkle over the almonds. Bake in the oven for 25 minutes, until golden.

Allow to cool in the tin before removing and cutting into 10 slices.

GINGER JELLY

This light dessert is perfect for those times when you want something a little sweet but not too indulgent. Change this up however you like by using whatever fruit you have as the mix-ins. Agar agar is a vegetable setting agent and is available in health food stores or the Asian section of some supermarkets.

1 x 10cm piece of fresh ginger, peeled and grated

400ml water

2 tbsp agar agar

½ tsp ground cinnamon

6 tbsp maple syrup

½ a pear, peeled, cored and diced

100g fresh or frozen raspberries

Put the ginger, water, agar agar and cinnamon in a saucepan over a medium heat and simmer for 2 minutes.

Bring to the boil, then lower the heat and simmer for 3 to 4 minutes, stirring occasionally, until the agar agar has dissolved. Remove from the heat and stir in the maple syrup with a whisk (not an electric one).

Spoon into four small jars or one 500ml jar, then add the diced pear and raspberries, which will float on the top. Place in the fridge for about 45 minutes to set. This keeps for up to four days in the fridge.

LEMON LIME MOUSSE

A zingy, refreshing, creamy dessert. I especially love this served with
some shortbread biscuits (page 213) for dipping into the mousse.

*2 x 400ml tins of
    full-fat coconut milk*

zest and juice of 1 lemon

*2 limes (zest of 1 and
    juice of 2)*

150ml water

2½ tbsp agar agar

5 tbsp maple syrup

To serve:

coconut yogurt

fresh mint leaves

Put the tins of coconut milk in the fridge for 45 minutes to
let the cream rise to the top and harden. Without shaking
the tins, open them up and scoop the hard white coconut
solids off the top – you need 8 tablespoons (4 tablespoons
from each tin) for this recipe. The cream will be hard, so put
it in a bowl and whisk until completely smooth using a hand-
held whisk.

Put the citrus zest and juice, water and agar agar in a saucepan
over a medium heat and simmer for 2 minutes. Bring to the
boil, then lower the heat and simmer for 3 to 4 minutes,
stirring occasionally, until the agar agar has dissolved. Remove
from the heat and stir in the coconut cream and maple syrup
with a whisk (not an electric one). It will be a creamy liquid.

Spoon into four small jars. Place in the fridge for 1 to 2 hours
to set into a silky smooth mousse. This keeps for up to four
days in the fridge.

To serve, top with coconut yogurt and mint leaves.

PEANUT BUTTER
CHOCOLATE MOUSSE

This almost tastes like one of those mousse pots you used to buy as a kid from the fridge section of a supermarket. It's thick, creamy and oh so chocolaty. Plus it's so easy that you'll soon be making this on repeat.

350g silken tofu

2 tbsp peanut butter, plus extra to serve

1½ tbsp maple syrup

1 tsp vanilla extract

120g vegan dark chocolate, chopped

To decorate:

chopped vegan dark chocolate

1 tbsp chopped peanuts

Put the silken tofu, peanut butter, maple syrup and vanilla extract in a blender and blitz into a smooth purée.

Melt the chocolate in a heatproof bowl set over a saucepan of simmering water, making sure the water doesn't touch the bottom of the bowl. Once the chocolate is melted, let it cool for 5 to 6 minutes before stirring it into the tofu purée. Make sure the mousse is fully combined – it should all be a chocolate brown colour.

Divide the mousse between four ramekins, small jars or bowls. Place in the fridge for 30 to 40 minutes to set. This keeps for up to four days in the fridge.

Just before serving, add an extra spoonful of peanut butter on top, then scatter over some chopped chocolate and chopped peanuts.

PINEAPPLE, MINT AND LIME SORBET

When the sun makes a rare appearance in Ireland, it's time to whip up a batch of my favourite sorbet, even if it's still a bit nippy! Sorbets have become my go-to treat during the summer months. You can make this sorbet with almost any fruit that's been peeled, diced and frozen solid, so it's a perfect way to use up fruit that might be starting to turn or just to eat fruit in a different kind of way. The sweetness of the pineapple still comes through even after being frozen (freezing food usually makes it taste less sweet), but if you use other fruits, like berries or melon, you might need to add 2 or 3 tablespoons of maple syrup.

1 large ripe pineapple
6 fresh mint leaves
2 limes (juice of 2 and zest of 1)

Peel the pineapple and remove and discard the tough core, then dice the pineapple into chunks. Spread out on a baking tray lined with non-stick baking paper and place in the freezer for at least 3 hours, until frozen solid.

Place the frozen pineapple, mint and lime zest and juice in a food processor and blend until smooth. Serve immediately.

INDEX

ACKNOWLEDGEMENTS

This is my favourite book so far, made possible by a wonder team and editor whom I would be lost without. Books are hard work, but it's people like these who make them fun along the way, bringing the food to life and carefully curating a wonderful book.

Starting with a special thanks to the best food photographer, Jo Murphy, who has shot my last three books. We've been on this journey together. Jo always works extra hard and lets me squeeze in those extra shots.

To my friend and food stylist, Sarah Watchorn, who works with me year round on different projects. This is her first book and I'm so glad it was with me!

A big shout out to my kitchen team, Chloe Chan, Jade Delaney and Susan Willis, for making the heat in the kitchen a little less intense for me by helping prep over 30 recipes a day. They managed to make a colossal workload seem easy!

As always, a very special thank you to my copy-editor, Kristin Jensen, who has also worked on my two other books, making sure every step along the way has been fine-tuned. I always know that when an email comes in from Kristin, it's the beginning of a new chapter – literally!

Thanks to everyone at Penguin Random House who gave me the opportunity to write my third book (I still can't believe it), with a special high five to my editor, Claire Pelly, who always encourages me, allows me to be creative and is great fun on a shoot.

Thanks to my friends Seanie and Ruth from Finders Keepers for sending over vintage outfits for me to wear for my cover shoot.

And lastly, to all my testers out there – my family and friends who have been guinea pigs for all the recipes – thank you for helping me to choose the best of the best!